DISCIPLINE YOUR KIDS with

POSITIVE
PARENTING

DISCIPLINE YOUR KIDS with
POSITIVE PARENTING

A Practical Guide to Building
Cooperation and Connecting
with Your Child | **NICOLE LIBIN, PhD**

ILLUSTRATIONS BY ADAM HOWLING

**ROCKRIDGE
PRESS**

Interior and Cover Designer: Lisa Schreiber
Art Producer: Hannah Dickerson
Editor: Jed Bickman
Production Editor: Ruth Sakata Corley
Illustrations © Adam Howling, 2020
Author photo courtesy of Laura Johnston, Laura Grace Photography, 2019

ISBN: Print 978-1-64611-461-0 | eBook 978-1-64611-462-7
R0

TO ARIA,
for helping me be a better
parent and a better person.
I love you infinity heaps.

CONTENTS

INTRODUCTION

You are not alone.

When you find yourself yelling at your kids way more than you ever thought you would.

When you're running on empty and still feel like you aren't doing enough.

When you're exhausted by 7:30 in the morning because it takes superhuman strength to make sure your children are dressed, fed, and out the door with all the school stuff they need.

When you feel like you're failing as a parent after giving in and letting the kid have the iPad because you just needed a break.

When you feel overwhelmed because it's two hours past your kid's bedtime and they're still awake, out of bed, or on their phone after you've already talked to them, reasoned with them, raised your voice, and used every tool you know and a few you wish you didn't.

When you feel guilty for yelling and threatening punishment, like you promised you'd never do, because you're at the end of your rope and can't handle one more iteration of "Stay in your seat while you eat" or "Go to sleep!"

And you are not alone when, after the umpteenth argument about the same thing, you find yourself stressed and frazzled, muttering that there's got to be a better way.

There *is* a better way. A way that helps everyone in the house feel more respected and heard. A way with less yelling, fewer fights, and more connection. The bad news is that no one tells us about it when we become parents. The good news is that it's totally doable, reasonable, and possible . . . it just takes a bit of knowledge and some practice.

As a mindfulness educator and author, I spend much of my time thinking about and focusing on ways to find more ease and less stress (for myself and others). Yet, when I became a mom, there were many, many times it felt like all my training went out the window. Sure, practicing taking a breath, naming my emotions, or understanding that I didn't have to believe all my thoughts were great strategies, but I often felt utterly overwhelmed by the sheer volume of challenges involved in raising a child. My useful skills frequently fell by the wayside.

I didn't want to become a yelling rage machine, but it seemed like my daughter pushed every one of my buttons, including some I didn't even know I had: for instance, when she couldn't (or wouldn't) sleep, when the foods that were her all-time favorites one day were disgusting the next, when we had a full year during which she wasn't shy about her very strong preference for her dad over me, or when she could have given lessons in the art of the get-out-of-bed excuse (including, at age three, convincing a babysitter that she was permitted fresh fruit after bedtime). And these challenges don't even cover all the worries and fears that seemed to consume me, from how challenging breastfeeding was to what if she gets bullied in school to what if she's true to her seven-year-old word and never actually does move out of the house!

I wanted to be a good parent; I just wasn't sure how best to support and nurture my daughter amid so many stresses while still being a functional person and partner.

So, I did what any actor would do. I asked myself, What's my motivation? It's cliché, but actors frequently ask these questions when trying to work out how to play a scene:

- What's the goal I'm trying to achieve? (Motivation)

- What's in the way of me achieving my goal? (Obstacles)

- How am I going to get past the obstacles to achieve the goal? (Means)

It turns out my goal is simple, though definitely not easy. It's for my daughter to thrive. To help her become a healthy, compassionate, discerning, content, and respectful person (now and as she grows up) *without sacrificing my own well-being in the process.*

The obstacles are many. They include my stress and fatigue, reactivity and conditioning, and any unrealistic expectations I or others have placed on me. They include not having enough time or patience or being pulled in too many directions. (Sound familiar?) They also include her developing brain, with its greater focus on emotional reactivity and still-maturing ability to think rationally.

And the means . . . well, that's where positive parenting enters the scene. It's a philosophy and an approach that offers a way of setting children—and the adults who love them—up for success in the world.

Positive parenting is focused on the long game. Although most parents would delight in quieter households, this strategy is not about getting children to shut up in the moment.

If that's all we wanted, we would just shove a screen in front of them at every turn. Instead, it's about helping them flourish, thrive, and find their own way.

Positive parenting recognizes that the goal of parenting, for most of us, isn't to be a dictator. It's about being a guide. A teacher. Someone who makes it safe and possible for children to learn things on their own and make wise choices. It's a way of approaching our children and a particular situation by responding deliberately rather than reacting automatically. Sure, yelling (or screens) might be quicker or easier in the moment, but they are actually obstacles, not the means, to the goal.

Being a parent is hard frickin' work. Not just because we don't know what the hell we're doing a lot of the time. And not just because we aren't trained. And not just because the objects of all our hard work often can't sit still, speak only in grunts or eye rolls, or are singing "Baby Shark" at the top of their lungs for the nine hundredth time in a row. It's hard because it matters and we care so much. That's why you picked up this book. Because you care.

Now for the unfortunate truth: This book will not make all the challenges go away. It's not a panacea or magic bullet. It won't get rid of all the struggles. The techniques in this book definitely haven't made me a perfect parent—whatever that is. My walls have seen their fair share of permanent marker, bedtime continues to be a major battle, and our home is not immune to shouting matches or power struggles.

Following the approach outlined in these pages doesn't mean you have to change everything about yourself (or your children). You still get to be human, with its many joys, stresses, and challenges.

GETTING RID OF PERFECT

If you spend even a few moments researching parenting tips online, you'll probably come across many contradictory messages. You'll find all kinds of research on how stressed parents are because the demands of parenting are so high and perfectionistic. Yet those very same articles and sites simultaneously push these impossible standards. Case in point: *Time* magazine's October 2017 cover on this subject. The copy was about challenging the impossibly high standards placed on mothers, but the cover photo was a perfectly photoshopped, camera-ready model who fit society's views of beauty without an ounce of fat beneath her perfectly coiffed hair. Perfection is pushed even while it's being challenged.

Here's an experiment: Take a moment or two to bring to mind an image of a perfect parent. Is it someone who never yells? Someone who devotes all their time to their children or never gets upset? Maybe it's someone who has mastered the art of building pillow forts while simultaneously managing to get all their work (and their hair) done perfectly. Or someone who never has to order takeout or eat cereal for dinner?

As you bring this image to mind, notice how it makes you feel, particularly how your body feels, as you consider how you *are* versus this ideal picture of how you *should* be.

Chances are, you'll notice some tightness in your chest or throat, some butterflies in your stomach, maybe some queasiness or discomfort.

Now, what happens if you tell yourself that it's okay to make mistakes? That, in fact, *every single person* makes mistakes and there are no perfect parents . . . just people like you who are doing their best. It's a bit easier to handle, right?

So, let's get this out of the way at the start: It is not possible to be a living, breathing, functioning parent and not lose it every once in a while. No one has unlimited patience. No parent is always ready with the right technique (or the wherewithal to think of one) in the moment.

This is good news. It means that we can cut ourselves a ton of slack and forgive ourselves when things go sideways. We don't have to feel ashamed for not being able to reach some sort of impossible standard. And it means that instead of striving for perfection, we can focus on reality. We get to see this whole parenting thing as an ongoing process of discovery and exploration. We get to keep asking ourselves what our children really need and what's really going on beneath their frustrating behaviors. We get to explore how we can help them and ourselves get where we all need to go . . . messy hair and all.

You still get to say no, set boundaries, and enforce the rules. The goal is to have real-world tools to be able to support the whole family, regardless of the inevitable conflicts and challenges.

Your children aren't going to stop asking to wear their tiger costumes to school or insist that they don't need coats when it's freezing outside. No matter what, we can't prevent them from assuring us that their homework is done when it's not or from forgetting their gym stuff at home. Kids are just doing what kids do.

The exercises and strategies in this book are designed to help you tackle parenting challenges in a way that makes sense to you. This book is not a manual but rather a guide to assist you in finding tools to make lasting changes for your family, leading to more confidence, less stress, and more ease overall.

But please don't just take my word for it. Try it out for yourself. One of the underlying ideas of positive parenting is to find what works for you by trusting your own body, mind, and heart while being open to change and new ideas, recognizing that you don't have to have all the answers.

What's in the Book

The book starts with an exploration of the core principles and qualities of positive parenting. We will explore its origin, how it differs from other models of parenting, how it relates to your own goals, and why it benefits the whole family in the long run.

Next, we will discuss how discipline fits into positive parenting, including the core principles of positive discipline and how it's distinct from punishment. We will then explore some of the key ideas, building blocks, and strategies of positive parenting before applying them to real-world scenarios and challenges.

Throughout the book, you will find exercises and suggestions to help you explore your own motivations, patterns, and expectations and uncover the means to overcome obstacles and support your parenting goals. You'll discover how our primary work as parents is to connect with ourselves first.

The goal is not about getting an A or doing everything perfectly, but rather finding the most supportive path for you and your family.

A Few Important Notes

First, although the approach is called positive parenting, our definition of "parent" is a broad one. The book is intended for anyone who cares for, nurtures, and guides children, regardless of your title or biological relationship.

Second, we all recognize that being a parent is tough work. The ideas and strategies in this book are here to support you, and sometimes, they won't be sufficient. If you are in a situation that feels especially debilitating, harmful, or dangerous (to you, your child, or other family members), please don't hesitate to seek professional help. You aren't alone, and you don't have to figure this out all by yourself. There is nothing wrong with reaching out for support.

If your children are demonstrating behavior that is harmful to themselves or others, please consult your doctor or therapist or consider one of the following resources:

- The American Academy of Child and Adolescent Psychiatry (aacap.org) includes lots of resources, fact sheets, and ways to get help.

- National Alliance for Mental Illness (nami.org) includes local support groups, a library of information and FAQs, and a help line (call 800-950-6264 or text NAMI to 741741).

- The Substance Abuse and Mental Health Services Administration (samhsa.gov/find-treatment) offers resources and helps families find treatment options. They have a free 24/7 hotline (call 1-800-662-HELP or text HELP to 4357).

Finally, if your child has a diagnosis such as autism, ADHD, or ODD, you should still find the ideas and techniques in this book helpful to support the work you are doing with professional therapists and doctors. There are also additional resources that speak to your child's needs and individual diagnoses.

CHAPTER 1

What Is Positive Parenting?

A while ago, my husband and I had a parenting moment that felt like a breakthrough. We were visiting a computer store at the mall. As I looked around, my daughter started playing on one of the demo computers, discovering what she claimed to be The Greatest Game Ever Invented. It took more effort than I care to admit to get her to leave the store. Once we did, she couldn't stop asking about the game: "Can I have the game? Can you buy me the game? Please can I have the game? I *need* the game. Why can't I have the game?" As we drove back home, the demands became more and more insistent while the volume kept increasing. She persisted and we got frustrated.

We asked her to stop; she didn't. We told her she wouldn't get the game if she kept going; that didn't work. We yelled to no avail. Finally, my husband turned to her and asked her why she wanted the game: "You keep saying you need to have it. Tell us why you love it so much. What makes you so excited about it? What makes this game so wonderful?" And, while I don't quite believe it myself, that's all it took. The yelling stopped, the demands were curtailed, and she delightedly described the game to us. By the time we got home, she was happy, we were calmer, and no one had done or said anything they'd regret later.

What we did wasn't superhuman. It wasn't unique. It was positive parenting. And it was effective because it got us all focusing on what was positive rather than on what wasn't. Instead of trying to stop the runaway freight train that is a child's desires and demands, or getting too caught up in our own frustrations, we got to encourage her in a way that was healthier for all of us. It was a way that focused on the qualities we wanted to cultivate (her enthusiasm, discernment, and communication skills) rather than the qualities that were problematic. Although this example is pretty tame compared to some of the things parents handle, the foundational ideas are the same.

Positive Parenting

Positive parenting is all about empowerment: empowering our children to develop skills and strengths that will support them throughout their lives, and giving them opportunities to hone and practice those skills and strengths. But it's not just for them. Positive parenting empowers parents, too, because it helps us choose how we want to respond in any given moment rather than simply reacting on autopilot. It helps us use discipline as a teaching tool focused on long-term goals rather than using punishment focused on short-term consequences. With an approach based on mutual respect, clear boundaries, trust, empathy, and awareness, everyone in the household can be empowered to flourish and thrive.

Where Does Positive Parenting Come From?

Positive parenting gets its main values, theories, and approaches from the discipline of positive psychology. Positive psychology emerged in the past few decades when several psychologists realized that the field of psychology was really only paying attention to what was wrong with us. There wasn't any focus on the science of happiness and human well-being. So, Martin Seligman and a few others started exploring human flourishing.

Positive psychology is the scientific study of what makes us thrive. The field explores positive states such as gratitude, compassion, and hope, focusing on our strengths rather than our weaknesses and ills. It's not about making people happy all the time or ignoring bad stuff when it comes up. Instead, it's about uncovering what we need to feel good about ourselves, each other, and the world around us.

Like positive psychology, positive parenting shifts the focus from getting rid of what's wrong to paying attention to what's right. So instead of just avoiding the bad, we get to focus on encouraging the good. Instead of all the instances of "Don't" and "Stop that right now," and "If you do that one more time," positive parenting focuses on positive instructions. It features approaches such as brainstorming solutions together, exploring the root of particular behaviors, and recognizing that kids aren't misbehaving as a means to make us angry. Positive parenting recognizes that our job isn't (just) to get rid of problems but to help our children thrive.

What Positive Parenting Is Not and Common Questions

Let's get some of the major myths and misconceptions out of the way before we really dive in.

Q. *Does focusing on the positive mean I have to give my kids whatever they want?*

A. Definitely not! Most of us have been around children (adults, too) who have never heard the word no. It's not a pretty sight and does not promote overall well-being. Positive parenting is about making choices in the moment that will lead to positive states in the long run.

Q. *This sounds very Pollyanna-ish, too optimistic and happy. What's the deal?*

A. Positive does not mean happy. It also doesn't mean pleasant. Positive parenting does *not* mean that everything will feel good all the time or that we ignore or gloss over the negative. It's not a state we are trying to reach but an overall approach that focuses on positive goals and the means to achieve those goals.

Q. *So, if I follow this book, it means my child will behave?*

A. Sorry, no. Although these techniques can be extremely effective, they still take work and they still operate in the real world. Children aren't robots; they tend not to follow what we want, definitely not immediately. And neither do our own minds, really. Anyone who's ever tried to adopt a new habit knows that life and old habits get in the way at some point. And we will all still have moods, emotions, and bad days. We're not trying to get rid of who we are; we're just trying to keep the focus on what will support everyone overall.

Furthermore, this approach asks us to move beyond simply getting our children to behave. Sometimes their "misbehavior" is actually a demonstration of their strengths or passions. Sometimes it's a symptom of their dysregulated nervous systems (i.e., too many stimuli or emotions and not enough ability to manage it all). Misbehavior can also be an indication of something else that's happening, and many times, it's more about what we as parents can or cannot handle in the moment.

Q. *So, now I need to learn a whole new way of taking care of my kid?*

A. Nope. This is meant to support what you're already doing and perhaps help during those times when you just don't know what to do or are at the end of your rope. You get to decide what to listen to, what to try, and what to throw away. It comes down to what's meaningful and important to you and your family.

Q. *This feels impossible. Say something that will make me feel better.*

A. Okay. By picking up this book, you've already made it clear that you care, that you want your child to thrive, and that you're open to ideas and suggestions. Just like GI Joe said, "Knowing is half the battle." You've already taken a huge step with good intentions, openness to new ideas, and awareness that you can always keep learning. Remember that you're helping your children flourish and also helping yourself become not just a more positive parent but also a more contented person because you're promoting the well-being of the whole family.

Various Types of Parenting

In order to see where positive parenting fits, it's helpful to take a quick detour into other styles of parenting.

The most commonly recognized parenting styles—authoritative parenting, authoritarian parenting, and permissive parenting—were identified in the late 1960s by Diana Baumrind, a researcher at UC Berkeley. Subsequent researchers added one additional category, the neglectful parent, and created two sets of qualities that define these parenting styles: demanding/undemanding and responsive/unresponsive. This resulted in four basic parenting types:

Authoritative: strict rules with lots of room for maneuvering amid those boundaries; demanding and responsive.

Authoritarian: parent is boss, child follows; high expectations, more punishment; demanding and unresponsive.

Permissive: few rules, fewer punishments. Not a neglectful parent, but one more likely to see themselves as the child's friend rather than the authority figure; undemanding and responsive.

Neglectful: uninvolved, perhaps to the point of abuse; undemanding and unresponsive.

More recent styles have become more specific.

Free-Range: coined by a parent who opted to let her nine-year-old son find his own way home on the New York City subway system; greater autonomy and agency with rules still enforced.

Attachment: gained prominence in the 1980s through the work of William Sears, promoting the attachment of parent and child through emotional connection plus physical proximity and touch; attachment parenting aficionados are more likely to promote extended breastfeeding, baby wearing, and co-sleeping.

Helicopter/Overparenting: parents "hover" with overprotective natures; likely to be highly involved in their children's lives, offering little autonomy; good intentions may lead to disrupting the child's opportunities for growth and independence.

One note on these parenting styles: The values and approaches of different cultures haven't always been considered or represented by Western researchers, thus these styles may not be representative of global parenting approaches. Positive parenting finds itself largely in the authoritative category: demanding and responsive. It might take cues from free-range parenting with greater autonomy if that's a key quality those parents seek to foster.

EXPLORING YOUR OWN GOALS AND OBSTACLES

Those of us interested in positive parenting find the approach meaningful because it mirrors our own values. In this section, take some time to make these values explicit as you check out what's meaningful to you with respect to human flourishing. Next, you'll consider some of your own obstacles that might hinder those goals. Finally, we'll explore how those two pieces interact.

Take a moment to consider what you really want for your child(ren). What are your long-term goals? What qualities or strengths do you want to nurture in them? What tools would you like them to have when they're faced with difficult situations? How do you want them to treat other people?

_____

_____

_____

_____

_____

_____

_____

_____

_____

_____

_____

_____

_____

_____

_____

_____

_____

_____

_____

_____

_____

_____

_____

_____

_____

_____

_____

_____

_____

_____

_____

Now consider your obstacles. What might (or does) get in the way of working toward or achieving those goals?

_____

_____

_____

_____

_____

_____

_____

_____

_____

_____

_____

_____

_____

_____

_____

_____

Looking at the second list, chances are what came up were things like stress, not having enough time, losing your patience, being tired . . . life, basically.

The problem is that the obstacles are relatively unavoidable for us as parents. It's not like we're magically going to stop rushing everywhere (at least I'm not) or that our kids are always going to do their homework. Toddlers aren't going to stop having tantrums in the middle of supermarkets, and teenagers won't avoid making foolish choices (because their brains are actually wired that way). All this is part of parenting because it's part of growing up. And yet it also seems to get in the way of our good intentions.

It's like our short-term frustrations and our long-term goals are fighting with each other.

OBSTACLES AS OPPORTUNITIES

Here's the thing: We can't get rid of those obstacles, but we can change how we relate to them. Positive parenting asks us to see obstacles as opportunities that can help us reach those goals rather than obstacles that thwart them. The obstacles aren't actually in your way . . . they are your way. (Yeah, I groaned at that one, too.)

Being aware of goals and obstacles is the start. We can't change our relationship to the obstacles until we know they exist. We can't use the goals as guiding principles unless they are clear.

But we're not going to stop everything to focus on big life lessons. As parents, we likely spend more time stuck in traffic than we do in deep conversation. So, if we wait for special or calm moments to reach our long-term goals, we'll probably be waiting a long time. Most positive parenting happens in the little, everyday moments. It starts with how we approach our children.

Key Qualities of Positive Parents

Check out these qualities and see what resonates. What is most important to you as you seek to connect with and nurture your children?

Awareness and Acknowledgment: These really are the foundations of this approach. You can't change or respond to what you aren't aware of or don't acknowledge. This includes acknowledging what is true or challenging for you in the moment and also what is true or challenging for your child. One of the first things a positive parent should be doing is asking, What's really going on here?

Empathy: We all have our own expectations, but our children need us to do our best to see things from their perspectives. Yes, it's true that I paid quite a bit for my daughter to take circus classes (and yes, that's a real thing). It's also true that the class was really hard, and she was struggling with it. Ignoring or dismissing her concerns would only belittle her feelings or dissuade her from being honest in the future (neither of which I wanted).

Sensitivity: Connected to empathy and awareness, sensitivity is about attuning to what's really going on for them. Even if your automatic reaction to your child saying she doesn't like her classmate is "Of course you do! You're best friends," she needs you to be sensitive to what she's feeling at that time. Maybe there's more to the story or maybe she's just having a tough afternoon. Either way, being sensitive and really listening helps build connection and trust.

Mindfulness: A current buzzword, mindfulness can be defined as present-moment awareness leading to the ability to respond deliberately to what's happening with kindness and nonjudgment. Mindfulness allows us to check our own judgments or frustrations before saying something we might regret or getting stuck in parent-as-rage-monster mode.

Flexibility: It's easy to get frustrated because our children aren't doing what we want or expect when we need something done. Getting annoyed might feel automatic after you've asked your son for the thirteenth time to make his bed. It's helpful to remember that neither being a parent nor being a child comes with scripts to follow. Instead, they're more like an improvisation where we just keep listening and connecting to what the other person is offering. We want to model flexibility because we want to nurture our children to be open to new ideas and new ways of doing things rather than rigidly following all orders.

Patience: Although we want things done quickly, patience is essential, not only as a model for something we want our kids to emulate, but also as a vital skill for parents. This is where learning about what's going on in our children's brains can be really helpful. Developing brains truly can't switch from one task to another as fast as we would like them to. Teenage brains don't make poor decisions on purpose. Patience gives us extra time to see what's happening in any given situation and allow for more space before we jump in or react.

Respect: Again, this comes back to those long-term goals. We want our children to be respected and respectful as they grow up. The best way to foster that is to demonstrate it, toward them and others. Show them what it means to listen to someone else's ideas, even if you disagree. This isn't saying that the opinion to have marshmallows for dinner holds equal weight with the balanced meal you've planned, but listening openly and respecting that they have ideas and are using their brains shows them that they and their ideas matter. Respect helps remind us to treat our children as people, not just as robots who follow our commands.

Trust: If we want our kids to be trustworthy, we have to trust them. That doesn't mean we let three-year-olds take the subway alone. But if we give them the chance to exercise their own agency, they will build this skill. We create the conditions for them to be able to try new things, fail, and pick themselves back up and try again.

Love: Perhaps it sounds obvious, but love really is the key to helping our kids thrive. Throughout all the frustrations and stresses, we keep coming back to our unconditional love for and commitment to our children. Even when we need (and deserve) a break from them, positive parenting is rooted in the idea that we will love our children and show them that love and warmth, no matter what.

Conclusion

The key to positive parenting is practice. You don't have to be innately good at being patient. (Really, who is?) But the more you keep these principles in mind, the more you try to incorporate them into your life, the better you will get at them. Remember the first time you put a diaper on your baby or walked down the stairs holding them? That probably felt a bit awkward and scary. (Okay, the stairs thing felt truly terrifying.) But after you do it for the five thousandth time, it's not a big deal. It's the same thing here: The more you practice these qualities, the more automatic they become. Neuroscience research is demonstrating this more and more. It's called neuroplasticity: the idea that our brains change based on our environments and experiences. By paying attention in a particular way (say, really focusing on patience or practicing concentration) you can rewire the networks in your brain. Just like building muscles at the gym, the more you practice any particular habit, the better your brain gets at it.

Step one is taking a breath and knowing that you are doing great. You have not irrevocably screwed up your child (or yourself) because you weren't doing this stuff before. You've already been building and demonstrating the qualities that will serve you best. Positive parenting just encourages you to be a bit more deliberate about the whole thing.

Gratitude fits in perfectly with other positive parenting qualities. It helps us support our children by fostering an environment that will help the whole family prosper. It, too, becomes more natural the more we practice it. Research shows that gratitude promotes mental and physical well-being and boosts overall happiness and connection with others.

To practice gratitude, all you need is the intention to notice what's happening and to look for anything in that moment that you can appreciate. It can be helpful to create a daily ritual where you pause, take a breath, and contemplate three to five things that you appreciate, that make you happy, or for which you are grateful. They can be big, such as your family's good health, or tiny, such as a second of quiet during that first sip of coffee. Try to give yourself a moment or two to really soak in those feelings before going about the rest of your day.

It's helpful to write down or share your gratitude with friends or family members. One of my favorite practices in our house is the use of "gratitude jars." They're just glass jars that each family member decorated. We keep small slips of paper on which everyone writes what made them grateful that day, and we place them in the jars to remind us of all that we are grateful for.

CHAPTER 2

What Is Discipline, Really?

OR, WHAT'S MY ROLE AS A PARENT?

S creen time. It's a hot topic in most households. Not just because it causes so much controversy (How much is too much? Is it safe? Why is Dora the Explorer that particular shade of orange?) but because it's the source of so many heated battles.

My husband and I have always been pretty strict with screen time. I'm not sure if it backfired or if this would have happened anyway, but for a long time, whenever my daughter did get to watch something, it ended up in a serious meltdown. Lots of frustration and pleading, with frequent door slamming and tears. You can imagine the not-so-pretty picture.

I knew yelling about the meltdown didn't work because she would just get angrier and yell back. I also understood her perspective. She loves being entertained (who doesn't?) and she would get caught up in the excitement of the show and not want to stop. But how could I get her to accept that she could watch one show only without life erupting into some sort of doomsday apocalypse?

One day, when we were both calm, we sat down to talk about it.

Me: Lovey, I notice that every time you watch a show, we end up having a tough time. Can you tell me about it?

Her: I always want to watch more. You never let me. Shows are longer than you give me, and I always have to turn it off right in the middle.

Me: Okay. I hear you. That sounds very frustrating. Now, what do you think we should do about it?

Together, we wrote down a list of all the possible solutions, keeping in the craziest ideas (she quits school, I quit work, and we only watch TV all the time) as well as the ones that were a bit more realistic. I knew I didn't want to be yelling. I also knew that I wanted to give her more independence and opportunities to exercise her own decision-making abilities and agency; I knew she could handle it. Together we decided that she would have five (22-minute) shows a week. On her own, she devised a system where she puts one of five marbles in a cup each time she watches a show. When the marbles are done, there are no more shows that week. Now it's up to her to decide how to allot her TV time.

It's been amazing—not without any issues, of course, but night and day compared to what it was. This plan meant that my husband and I could stop policing her. The frustration, pleading, and yelling have (mostly) stopped, too. Even better, she is practicing all sorts of good habits: being responsible, budgeting limited resources, being in charge of her own time, and decision making. We are all a lot happier about the situation.

What's My Role as a Parent? Guide, Not Dictator

It's pretty misleading to offer this example of positive parenting as if it all comes naturally, as if I hadn't been terribly frustrated and done everything but this a hundred times before. After much contemplation, I believe the key reason our marble jar worked was because I changed my role in the exchange. Instead of being the enforcer, I was the guide. Instead of needing to solve the problem when everyone was feeling aggrieved, I waited until we could figure it out together, as two human beings with needs, feelings, and struggles. As cheesy as all this sounds, it meant that we worked together to find the solution.

With positive parenting, we still provide warmth and security, still create boundaries, and still nurture and care. What we are asked to reconsider is how we approach and interpret our children's behavior, especially misbehavior. If we see every unexpected thing our kids do as a problem that needs to be fixed, we are all going to end up very unhappy very quickly, parents and children alike. They would never be able to live up to such impossible standards, and we'd always feel like failures for not being able to enforce them. We need to get away from the idea of trying to fix our children, corral them, or make them behave in the way we've decided they should. Not that there aren't rules to follow; structure is still vitally important, and we still get to enforce that structure. But we don't want blindly obedient robots (as appealing as that idea might seem at times). We want to nurture them as human beings. We are their guides, not their task masters, chauffeurs, police, or stage managers, even if all that stuff is sometimes part of the job.

Positive Discipline Versus Punishment

As every article, blog, or book on this subject will tell you, the root of the word "discipline" is more connected to teaching and learning than to punishment. Although discipline and punishment have become almost synonymous, the differences between the two approaches are vast. They differ in motivation, approach, mindset, techniques, and outcome. So, basically everything.

Discipline is intended to be instructive and constructive. It's responsive in that the person applying the discipline sees what has happened and is happening and responds consciously in a way that trains for the future.

Punishment is reactionary. Rather than responding on purpose, the person applying the punishment is doing so automatically and often not consciously. Punishment is about invoking negative consequences based on past behavior. It isn't always, but it can be quite destructive instead of constructive. Applying punishment is offering a negative stimulus (or taking away a positive one) in order to eliminate an undesirable behavior.

Discipline looks forward to a different outcome. It's positive, never punitive, though still firm.

Punishment is not future-oriented or progressive and focuses only on what happened in the past.

STAYING GROUNDED IN YOUR LONG-TERM GOALS

Ultimately, discipline is a part of positive parenting because it helps our children thrive in the long run by fostering critical and creative thinking, engagement, responsibility, and compassion. Discipline encourages healthy brain development by letting our children make mistakes without fear of reprisal, learn from those mistakes, forgive themselves, and try new things. It also helps our children find intrinsic motivation to act in the world, so they aren't doing something just because we ask for it. That means they are more likely to keep doing it even when mom's or dad's eyes aren't watching. Because punishment focuses only on misbehavior, it can actually promote the habits it seeks to curtail: dishonesty to avoid punishment in the future, less connection between parent and child, and the child internalizing the punishment and condemning themselves, not just the behavior.

If you feel like punishment is easier, you're right. It is easier, at least in a way, because it's reactive and automatic rather than responsive and deliberate. When someone hits you, your system reacts automatically. Your heart pounds, your breath gets shallow, your body temperature rises, and you want to lash out. You get angry; you yell. Punishment uses that immediate reaction to punitive ends. Discipline, however, is all about responding. It's more measured, more deliberate, and more conscious. It considers the big picture. Short-term solutions like yelling, sarcasm, or punishment might be easier, but they likely aren't in line with your long-term goals.

Let's look at the example of getting our kids to make their beds without an argument. The task is important and helpful for our own sanity, but arguing about it only deals with the short term. We're trying to change how we relate to our children and such tasks. Consider why you want your daughter to make her own bed.

Options

A. Because I had to make my own bed, and it's only fair.

B. Because I had to make my own bed, and it sucked and she should feel that, too.

C. Because it's driving me crazy that the bed isn't made and that she's not listening.

D. Because it's important to learn responsibility and for her to take pride in her environment.

E. Because I want the house to be clean.

Your reason is probably some combination of (d) and (e), both of which are more about overall and long-term well-being rather than short-term solutions. But those reasons often get lost and we tend to get stuck on option (c) a bit too much. The bed isn't actually the main issue, and it's helpful to keep that in mind. As Shanker and Barker put it: "All too often we confuse our needs with the child's. We seek to make children more manageable, rather than self-managing."

WHY DO WE PUNISH?

Of course, making the bed isn't as important as some of the bigger challenges you'll face. Avoiding reacting or overreacting can be much harder for issues such as kids sneaking out, lying, tantrums in public, breaking things, cutting class, and/or not being respect-ful. But even those more challenging examples come back to the same things: You want your child to feel loved and safe, and you want to help them flourish. Want to ensure they continue to break the rules? Demand full obedience without listening to them and forbid them from seeing their friends or ever having their say. Now you've got a teen who still wants her independence but is just going to sneak behind your back to get it. Likewise, yelling is one of the surest ways to get a toddler or preschooler to keep having the tantrum (or get even louder).

Think of it this way: When you make a mistake at work, how do you want your boss or superior to respond? Consider your reaction to the following. Your boss

- yells at you, calls you names, and shames you.

- makes you sit at your desk until the task is complete and perfect, even though it's long past 6:00 p.m.

- keeps bringing up your mistake every time a new project comes up.

- demands that you sit in her office while you do your work so she can keep checking on you every minute.

Pissed off yet?

Each of these might make us complete the task, but we won't be motivated to put in the effort in the future; we'll just be resentful. Human beings make mistakes. A ton of them. All the damn time. Punishment only makes us feel bad and encourages us to cover up or hide our behavior. As one psychologist describes it, punishment makes us polite. It doesn't help us improve long term, nor does it intrinsically motivate us. Though the circumstances are different, the impact is the same with children. Punishment might make them polite (for a moment) but it won't help them or us in the long run.

If it's so bad, why would we punish our children?

One painfully honest answer is because we're stressed, and we get mad and frustrated and lash out. We might not want to admit it, but a lot of punishment comes as an automatic reaction based not on our conscious choices but our current emotions. Again, this is totally understandable. It's a natural human reaction, but that reaction isn't serving us or our kids. That's why positive parenting offers tools to help us overcome our automatic reactions and choose a more balanced response.

But choosing a more balanced response isn't necessarily intuitive. Our brains are naturally wired to react. As we discovered in chapter 1, kids become skilled in and more likely to imitate whatever we do repeatedly. The more we yell at our kids, the more well-worn and familiar that neural pathway becomes. Likewise, the more we practice patience, perspective, and choosing a measured response, the better our brains get at those and the easier they will be in the future.

There should definitely be rules and consequences, including serious consequences when necessary, for breaking those rules. But with positive discipline, the system is set up in advance and/or is considered thoughtfully in the moment. Discipline is about training, helping, and guiding our children toward positive behaviors rather than castigating them for misbehaviors.

Fear Versus Love

No matter what happens, we want to make sure our children know that we love them unconditionally. The message is: *I am disappointed and upset about what has happened **and** nothing could ever make me stop loving you.* Love-guided discipline lets our children understand that they are not inherently bad. Their behaviors might be troubling or less than desirable. Their actions might be wrong or upsetting, even painful for us. But our kids aren't bad people.

Children who are punished can become fearful of the punisher. Fear might masquerade as respect, but it's decidedly different. Fear is paralyzing. Children cannot learn new skills or ideas when they are overwhelmed with fear. With discipline, even the strictest discipline, we get to assure our children that we are coming from a place of love and that it's normal to make mistakes.

When we punish our kids, we are, in essence, trying to control them. When we discipline them, we are helping them learn to manage themselves. We want our motivation to be our love for them, just as they are. Positive parenting reminds us that love is at the heart of everything, rather than fear, control, or needing to get it "right."

What Doesn't Work and Why Not?

On one level or another, most of us know that punishment doesn't work, at least not in the way we want. When children get punished for not doing their homework, for example, it often leads to resentment ("I'll show them") rather than reform ("I'll do better next time"). When you punish your kid for hitting his brother, the lesson is just as likely to be "I'll be sneakier at it next time" as "I really shouldn't do that." Sadly, there's a whole host of other parenting tactics that fail us in similar ways. Here, we'll explore why some of our usual approaches may not be the optimal way forward.

THREATS

Threats fail because they are all about fear. They promote fear of a negative consequence rather than encouraging children to find their own ways forward. Threats mean that we are exerting control (or trying to) over our kids rather than helping them control and regulate themselves. Threats can ruin the child's internal motivation. Children then learn to fear consequences and are less likely to explore new things and more likely to argue.

Threats also fail because we often don't follow through on them. Not only do children need consistency, they very quickly learn our patterns. If we threaten and don't act, children know there is no consequence and therefore no reason to change the behavior.

SARCASM

I'm all for a good sarcastic retort, but this backfires on parents because the last thing we want is a six-year-old sassing us back. It's not a quality we want to help them build (not that they really need our help with that, anyway). Sarcasm comes from a very honest place: usually our own reactivity and frustration. It often makes itself known when we just don't know what else to do or have no more patience or resources. But sarcasm undermines what the child is experiencing. It invalidates their real feelings.

I have a painful example of this. I was seven years old and learning a second language. I must have had quite a bit of difficulty with it because a common refrain out of my second-grader mouth was "I don't get it." I wasn't trying to be obtuse; I just had trouble understanding. One day, I went to my teacher to ask a question and before I could she said, "Let me guess, you don't get it." My heart sank. To this day, that memory is painful because an adult made fun of me, an admittedly overly sensitive child. Although I can certainly understand that the teacher might have been at the end of her rope, with few resources and limited patience for 30 seven-year-olds, her quick retort has stuck with me for decades.

REWARDS

This one just doesn't seem fair. Rewards are positive, right? There can't possibly be anything wrong with those. Yeah, sorry. One parenting expert even calls rewards and punishments "two sides of the same coin."

The main issue is that rewards mean that the behavior becomes about getting something, rather than doing it for its own sake. Rewards can undermine intrinsic motivation. Instead of promoting self-reliance, responsibility, integrity, or other qualities you might have discovered in chapter 1, you're actually promoting the external prize. And once the reward is established, you might have to keep upping the ante. Parents who are familiar with children asking something like "If I do this, what will you give me?" know this too well. Rewards can also mean that children refuse to do an action if they won't get something for it.

It's not that you can't ever use external rewards, but experts suggest using them sparingly, so the focus is on internal motivation rather than external prizes.

One final, important note on this: We, like our kids, are human. We, like our kids, make mistakes. Just like them, we want to be seen, heard, and forgiven. If—no, *when*—you threaten, or use sarcasm, or offer a reward, it's not the end of the world. You have not screwed everything up. You made a mistake. This is actually an opportunity to model healthy behavior for your children. Let them see that people make mistakes all the time and that the healthiest, most mature thing to do is to see those mistakes, make amends (including apologizing to them if needed), forgive yourself, and move on.

Children Model Our Behavior

We all know that no matter what we say, our children are paying attention to what we do. They learn from watching us. (Anyone else ever overheard their preschooler swearing because they heard it from you? While it's kind of adorably inappropriate to hear a three-year-old say f**k, it isn't something most of us would choose.)

It's helpful to take a moment to consider what you really want to pass on to your children and what you would rather keep to yourself or, more likely, eliminate entirely. How do you want your child to communicate with other people? Their siblings? Teachers? Friends? How do you hope they will talk to themselves? What are you modeling?

One prime example of this modeling is body image. It's rare to find anyone without some sort of hang-up about their body. And it's a pretty safe bet that no one would wish those hardships on their children. Yet, the more we make a big deal about our own body image challenges, the more they learn that these behaviors are normal. This goes back to the basic notion that we are trying to build skills and qualities that will support their long-term flourishing. Instead of hearing us say how much we hate our bodies, we try to model strength and confidence: *I love how my legs help me run long distances. I'm so proud of my powerful body that let me give birth to you.* (And who knows, maybe if we say it enough to model for them, we might actually start believing it ourselves.)

This is how positive parenting makes every moment an opportunity. If we yell at them, they learn that yelling is okay. This means they might yell back but they also might turn around and yell at someone at school or on the playground. In its most extreme example, this is how the cycle of abuse begins. For most of us, it just means walking the walk.

IN CASE THIS MAKES YOU FEEL BAD

Some parents are able to read a book like this, take what works for them, discard what doesn't, and proceed. Then there are those of us for whom, no matter how much we tell ourselves otherwise, a book like this can make us feel bad. I know this because when I was researching for the book, page after page of what I read made me anxious. *What have I been doing? I'm a terrible parent. I'll never be able to master this stuff.* If this doesn't sound familiar to you, feel free to skip this section. If it does, you are not alone. No matter how we got here, some of us are more likely to see the negative more than the positive, to see all that we've done "wrong" instead of all that we are doing right. This negativity bias is actually something that's naturally built into everyone's brain. Humans are wired to see the bad more than the good. We *will* remember our mistakes, their tantrums, and family arguments more because that's how the human brain works. It's not bad. It does mean that we need to work a bit harder (or a lot harder at times) to focus on what is working rather than rely on our brains to filter it for us.

If you find yourself in this position, again, there is nothing wrong with you. It's helpful to check in and notice these patterns. The more familiar they become, the less likely they are to jump up and bite us in the ass. Some of us just need to remind ourselves of all that we are doing right, of how our children are thriving and how they are loved. Sure, we still have arguments about teeth brushing, and yes, those arguments are more memorable when we're doubting ourselves or when we are tired or stressed, but that's not the whole picture.

It's really helpful to look at the long view when doubts and fears creep in. The evidence shows that our children are prospering despite our temporary shortcomings. Even if it feels like potty training has gone on forever, we can trust that our children won't be in diapers when they're in college.

So, if this book does make you feel bad or have doubts, know that it's okay. It's just your brain doing its thing. And you can do something about it. You don't have to be a slave to negativity bias. It's a matter of recognizing and reminding yourself that your brain isn't giving you the whole story. In fact, the more you practice focusing on the good, the more your brain will give it attention, helping you develop a more balanced perspective.

Conclusion

The conversations and ideas presented in this book are designed to be an ongoing exploration. If we expect ourselves to get it immediately or drop all the unhelpful habits we've accumulated for years overnight, we're setting ourselves up for failure. Consider starting by picking one thing that you're going to focus on. Right now, for me, it's trying to stop controlling everything that happens in our house on weekday mornings. I'm trying to give my daughter more freedom and help her choose her priorities and build her capacity for responsibility. I'm not necessarily good at it, but that's okay. It's just about having the intention and doing our best to follow through.

SELF-CARE BREAK: Timed Breath

Doing a timed breathing exercise is a simple way to give yourself a break and trigger a relaxation response. The key is to make your exhalation longer than your inhalation. Doing this stimulates nerves that signal our parasympathetic nervous response (rest and digest mode). It tells your system that it's safe to calm down.

Try this: Wherever you are, take a moment to notice how your body feels, consciously letting go of any tension. As you notice the feeling of breathing, focus on making the out-breath even just one count longer than the in-breath. Either by whispering or counting in your head, breathe in for a count of four and out for a count of five to eight. (Fun fact: If you take your pulse during this exercise, you can actually feel your heart rate slow down on the out-breath.)

CHAPTER 3

It Starts with You

A s I was preparing to write this book, I started to pay more attention to my own parenting and, in particular, when things went off the rails. I never want to get aggravated or yell at my daughter. Those do not fit with my objectives, nor are they tools that I want in my arsenal. And yet, there they are. I would ask her to brush her teeth and, like any grade-school child, she'd get distracted and start building Lego, making me frustrated that she wasn't listening. Or, I'd be relieved that my day was over and eager to chill on the couch for a bit and she'd be out of bed with something she just *had* to tell me. I wouldn't yell every time but there was definitely an ongoing issue with volume and stress.

As I looked more closely at my reactions, I started to notice a pattern that was telling and also quite humbling. To put it simply, my stress level dictated my reaction.

(You'll have to excuse the crude depictions: I'm a writer, not a graphic designer. But I think the results speak for themselves.)

Throughout, my daughter remained the same. My level of yelling had far less to do

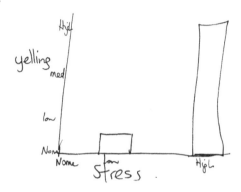

with what she was doing and infinitely more with how I was feeling. When I had a better day or was more rested, I had more patience and could choose how I responded to her. When my stress level was high or I was tired or grumpy, I was more likely to lose my carefully honed parenting tools and become a yelling machine.

My tools of discipline were *directly related* to my own mood and frame of mind.

Here's an uncomfortable truth: We can't control our kids. And while we know this, somehow, this sneaky little thought keeps worming its way back into our consciousness: *If I just repeat myself again or raise my voice to just the right tone, they will do what I say immediately.* Not exactly a reliable method. We can't control their tantrums, their joys, their sleeping, or their growth rate. We can't control most of the situations in which they find themselves. We can do our best, but we aren't actually in charge of the bad grades or the mean friends, the gossip or the trends in society.

We can't control most of our own situations, either. We aren't in charge of the weather, traffic, or the price of food. We aren't really even in control of most parts of ourselves. Think about it: We have something like 50 thousand to 100 thousand thoughts each day. How many of those do we actually ask for? Very few of us would choose to be stuck thinking the same damn thought at three in the morning. How often are we really in control of our emotions? Anyone else ever feel like your emotions are actually controlling you? Or you can't help worrying even when you know worrying doesn't help? Even our bodies aren't entirely in our control.

The primary thing we **can** *control is how we respond.* We often don't choose what's happening, but if we can see it, we can choose how we respond to it. And that can change everything.

Put on Your Own Oxygen Mask First

The first step of taking care of our children is actually taking care of ourselves. The oft-repeated airplane instructions make this clear: Put your own oxygen mask on before helping others. We can't help anyone else if we haven't first helped ourselves.

This can be hard for parents or guardians because our instinct is to tend to our children first. We put their needs before ours and we are even shamed or called selfish for doing anything but. No wonder so many of us feel bad about taking time for ourselves. But caring for ourselves is not selfish. It's a basic human need and right. If that isn't reason enough, it's also the only way we can really care for our children.

SELF-REGULATION

This makes sense when we consider that the human nervous system is a collective one. You know this from experience. If one person comes into a room in a major panic, it becomes hard not to react to that panic. When someone else is really excited, you feel excited, too. Humans regulate their nervous systems to each other.

This is most obvious when our children are infants. Remember all that time you spent rocking, shushing, holding, swaying, talking softly, and touching them gently but firmly enough so they felt secure and safe? We do this in order to regulate their nervous systems. For the most part, babies can't self-soothe. Much of the time, our children co-regulate their nervous systems with ours. We can support them to find balance when they've lost it, but we can only do this when our own systems are regulated.

I remember a time when my daughter was a few weeks old (admittedly, the memory is hazy but I swear it's there). I was overtired, hormonal, and stressed. She wouldn't stop crying for what felt like hours, and to be honest, I couldn't either. The more upset she got, the more upset I got. And vice versa, so it seemed. Luckily, I had help. Within minutes of my husband taking her, the crying stopped and she was fine. (And after a long shower and a break, I was, too.) I just didn't have it in me at the time to be able to soothe her.

Furthermore, current research is demonstrating that our happiness may actually be collective. Eminent social network researchers James Fowler and Nicholas Christakis determined that happiness spreads between connected individuals and groups. That doesn't mean that your child needs you to be happy all the time or that your child needs to make you happy. It signals that taking care of our own health and well-being can make a difference for the people we love.

Caregivers cannot pour from an empty cup. If we are burnt out, it becomes almost impossible to offer real care to our children. If we're always in fight-or-flight mode, they will become increasingly agitated, too. Think of a field of white-tailed deer. When one hears a sound or senses something suspicious, its tail goes up. Almost immediately, all the other tails go up, too, until the threat passes, one way or another. When it comes to our kids, if we want their "tails" to be down, we can't come in with ours up. When our nervous systems are dysregulated, it's all too easy to pass that on to them.

This doesn't mean that you always have to be calm or you can go and get a million massages (sorry!). It just means that the first step in supporting your child is supporting yourself. It's taking a breath or two and checking your own nervous system before you help them, unless, of course, there is immediate danger.

This moment or breath will help you be more present and stable for your own life as well as for theirs. It will also make you less likely to react on autopilot or behave in a way that doesn't help at that moment.

Checking and regulating your own nervous system might be something you've never really thought about, but you've done it many, many times. Any time you've stopped and taken a breath, any time you needed some space and went for a walk, or any time you paused before saying something you might later regret, you've been self-regulating. Self-regulation is not about telling yourself to stop worrying or controlling yourself; it's much more—and much more realistic—than control. Self-regulation is recognizing and responding to stress and/or disruptive emotions and thoughts in a healthy, more supportive manner.

Mindfulness and Positive Parenting

The key to self-regulation is being aware of what's happening in the first place. One of the best ways to approach that is with mindfulness.

Though mindfulness can be defined in many ways, most definitions share key traits: present-moment awareness, nonjudgment, compassion, and curiosity. Mindfulness is a way of training the mind to be aware of what's happening as it's happening, with kindness and without judgment, so we can choose to respond to the present moment in the way we want rather than the way we respond habitually.

Mindfulness can't make all your problems go away. It won't get homework done faster and it won't put children to bed on time. But it's an essential part of positive parenting because it offers you some space in stressful situations so you can respond in a healthier, more supportive way. So when your six-year-old breaks yet another dish while carrying too many plates to the table, you can check your automatic (angry, frustrated, want to yell) reaction, see that they didn't do it on purpose, stop and take a breath, and decide how to respond in a way that is consistent with your long-term goals and appropriate for the situation.

BASIC SKILLS FOR MINDFULNESS

Mindfulness provides the foundation for positive parenting because it cultivates the ability to keep long-term goals in mind rather than getting caught up on short-term obstacles.

These are the main skills:

Present-moment awareness and focus. Anyone with children knows how easy it is to get caught up in worrying about the future or stuck in memories of the past. Mindfulness trains us to be aware of this very moment, helping us choose our focus at any given time.

Responding on purpose, with kindness. By seeing and acknowledging our automatic thoughts, feelings, and emotions, they lose their hold on us and we can choose a kinder, more supportive way to respond. This lets us take a break from our automatic, quick (and not always helpful) reactions and be with what's happening the way we choose.

Using our bodies as the anchor for our attention. We pay attention to what's happening in our bodies as a way to be with the present moment just as it is. Awareness of body sensations helps us let go of thoughts, judgments, and worries and allows us to use our breathing to regulate our nervous systems.

Being curious, nonjudgmental, kind, and compassionate. Mindfulness encourages us to let go of our preconceived judgments about why this moment should or shouldn't be the way it is and lets us respond to it with compassion.

For parents, the basic approach to mindfulness is

- seeing what's happening,

- seeing how our body and mind react automatically,

- pausing,

- breathing,

- connecting to the sensations in our body rather than the stories in our head,

- choosing a kind and deliberate way to respond that is grounded in

  » our long-term goals,

  » the structures and rules we've established previously,

  » our love, warmth, and caring.

Practicing mindfulness is like practicing any other skill: The more you do it, the easier and more habitual it will become. The more familiar you are with your own nervous system, body, emotions, and reactions, the more comfortable you will be when unpleasant things arise because you'll know what to expect and have the tools to respond.

Here are some practices you can try to help build this muscle.

BREATH AS ANCHOR

Connecting to breathing is one of the most supportive things you can do when everything feels out of control or overwhelming. Putting awareness on the physical sensations of breathing helps you let go of your current worries, thoughts, and plans and also gives you some space to choose how you want to respond to whatever is happening. It's like a reset button for the mind.

You can use connecting to your breath as a formal meditation practice, dedicating a specific space and time for it. You can also do it at any moment throughout your day when you need a pause and a reset.

GIVE IT A TRY: Connecting to Your Breathing

1. Find a position that feels comfortable for you right now, and take a few deep breaths, if that feels okay.

2. Next, let your breathing be natural and notice what it feels like to breathe.

3. Take a minute to scan through your body and let go of any obvious areas of tension. This isn't about forcing relaxation but just letting go where you can.

4. Turning your attention to your breath, try to be really interested in and curious about the physical sensations of breathing, what it feels like. You don't have to make your breath special or deep. There's no need to change it at all. Simply notice what it feels like. You can notice if it's smooth or choppy, long or short. Notice if you feel it more

in your nostrils, chest, or abdomen. Check out how it feels and moves.

5. Very quickly, you'll probably notice that your mind has wandered away. It's totally normal and expected. Whenever that happens, take a moment to notice where the mind goes. You can be kind and curious about that, too. Then gently bring your attention back to your breathing.

6. You aren't trying to get rid of your thoughts or have a blank mind. You're just trying to be curious about what's happening and be compassionate with yourself when your mind goes somewhere else.

7. Try to feel your breath as though you've never paid attention to it before.

8. When you're done, take a few more deep breaths and notice how you feel now.

This is a great exercise to share with your children to help them cultivate their own self-regulation tools. Every time you practice stopping and taking a breath, you are training your mind and helping your kids train theirs in a way that will help them for the rest of their lives. Your breath acts as an anchor for your attention. When your mind wanders off, being curious about and feeling your body breathe helps bring it back to right here, right now.

WHAT'S UNDERNEATH THE THOUGHTS?

Most parents get struck by some pretty terrible thoughts: *I'm a horrible parent. I'm never going to do anything right. I can't handle this. My kid will hate me forever.* The following practice is designed to help you see that thoughts aren't necessarily true or right (even if they feel like it in the moment) and that you don't have to believe them. The goal isn't to control your thoughts; it's to stop letting them control you. The way to do this is to notice what's really happening when a thought takes hold, and the way to do that is by paying attention to the process of thinking rather than the content of the thought. You get to practice seeing that you are not your thoughts and they don't have to define you.

In many Eastern cultures, thinking is another sense. Just like the ears hear sounds, the mind thinks thoughts. And just as we can let sounds come and go without needing to do anything about them or take them personally, we can try to do the same with thoughts.

GIVE IT A TRY: Exploring Your Thinking

1. Find a comfortable, upright posture and take a few deep breaths, checking out how you feel right now.

2. Let your breathing be natural. Spend a few moments letting your breath be your anchor. Allow your mind to focus on and notice the physical sensations of breathing.

3. When you notice that you are thinking, see if you can let those thoughts come and go without getting caught up in their story or content. You might imagine the thoughts

are clouds in the sky or even cars going by as you wait for the bus. You get to watch them pass without needing to do anything but notice.

4. It's natural and expected to get caught up in your thoughts, so you don't have to feel bad about it or feel like you can't do this exercise. Whenever you do notice you've been thinking, gently come back to the feeling of breathing and letting those thoughts come and go. As soon as you notice you're thinking, you're actually back in the present moment.

5. When thoughts won't simply pass or when you feel like you're stuck in thoughts or worries, see if you can explore *what it feels like* to have the thought instead of trying to get rid of it, diving into it, or beating yourself up for having it. Thoughts are usually closely connected to emotions and body sensations. Rather than getting caught up in the content of the thought, try to pay attention to what is happening in your body at that moment. What emotions are present? Where do you feel them in your body? Where do they start and end? How do they change as you watch them?

6. Every time you get caught back up in thinking or judging, try to let go of the story of the thought and come back to the physical sensations of this moment. Notice what your breath feels like. Notice everything you can about what you are feeling right now.

7. It doesn't matter if you have a million thoughts while you do this exercise. The idea is to see the thoughts for the ephemeral things they are and get curious about what's

really happening rather than trying to think your way through the thoughts or make them go away.

Remember: Thoughts aren't bad and you don't have to get rid of them. If you can see them, even if you see that you're really stuck in them, then you still get some space from that thought.

NAMING EMOTIONS

When we feel carried away by emotions, it's often because the amygdala (the alarm bell of the brain) is over-firing preventing the prefrontal cortex (the brain's CEO) from making rational, healthy decisions. Research shows that naming emotions helps decrease their power over us and re-engages the prefrontal cortex, letting us respond deliberately rather than feeling hijacked by our emotions or getting caught up in the thoughts that are fueling them.

GIVE IT A TRY: Feeling Your Feelings

1. Start by taking a few deep breaths and trying to be gentle with yourself. You might sit or lie still if that feels comfortable, or you can walk or move slowly instead. Use those deep breaths as a chance to reset and let go.

2. Allow your breath to be natural and notice how you feel right now.

3. Try to notice your feelings just as they are, without needing to stop or change them and without trying to figure out why they're there or what you're going to do about them.

4. When you're ready, gently ask yourself, What feeling is present right now?

5. You don't have to come up with the perfect answer. It doesn't even have to be a word. Just try to name something (aloud or in your head) that describes the feeling. It might be *anger, sadness, pissed off, green, gobbledy-gook*, or *bleh*.

6. Once it has a name, notice how it feels in your body. What does anger actually feel like? Where do you feel frustration? What temperature is annoyance?

7. As you do this, you might notice that the feeling changes *and* that your mind doesn't want to stay with your body. It's easy and natural to get caught up in thinking, blaming, or worrying. You can name those emotions or actions, too. The goal is to be gentle and kind to yourself as you notice and name what's going on.

8. When you feel ready, take another moment to notice and name how you feel now. You might take some more deep breaths before going about the rest of your day.

It's helpful to keep in mind that the point of these practices isn't to get rid of what's happening but to empower ourselves to change our relationship to it, if we want. You probably can't stop feeling upset, but with some awareness and compassion, you might be able to stop feeling upset *about* feeling upset.

Supporting Self-Regulation Through Self-Care

Self-care isn't selfish. It's vital for us as fully functioning human beings so we can a) have our own lives, passions, and goals not directly connected to our children, b) have regulated nervous systems both for ourselves and the people in our lives, and c) model self-care for our children. Although books like this one can offer suggestions, the truth is that you are the best person to figure out how to make this work for you and your family. You might take a moment to consider what you really need in order to take care of yourself. Is it more "me time" with less guilt? This time can be spent on anything from waterskiing to crossword puzzles, from yoga to going for a walk. Physical activities and getting outside are really helpful for self-care and self-regulation, as are social connections and support in whatever way best fits your needs.

There's another way to look at this: We want our children to build skills that will support their long-term well-being, right? Since they learn so much by watching us, consider the beautiful lesson you're teaching them when your children see you engaged in your own passions, taking the time to care for yourself, and pursuing your own interests. It teaches them that it's a normal (and wonderful) thing to have interests, passions, and goals.

Finally, a word of encouragement: self-care, like everything else, can become just one more thing for the to-do list. Then it's not really self-care; it's just fodder for parental guilt (like we need any more of that). Taking care of yourself means recognizing your own needs. You get to see that you cannot possibly do everything; you cannot possibly keep

THIS WON'T WORK SOME OF THE TIME

I've read a lot of parenting books since my daughter was born. Many seem to offer perfect examples where the child listens the first time, teenagers communicate openly, or parents say some magical phrase and the challenging behavior immediately stops. Then I tried the techniques on my child and they bombed spectacularly. She never responded the way the books said she would. I would diligently follow the instructions and she'd hate the approach. Instead of soothing her when things were heated, it would make her agitated. Instead of fostering connection between us, it would make things more difficult. The books all made it seem so damn easy. Parenting is not easy. To quote *The Princess Bride*, "Anyone who says differently is selling something."

No matter what we do, it often won't go the way we plan or expect.

Here's the truth: You can follow all the guidelines, be aware of goals and obstacles, regulate your nervous system, choose your response instead of reacting automatically, and sometimes it just won't take. Your kid will run away from you, slam the door, and say he never wants to see you again. You'll yell, lose your cool, or won't have the wherewithal to know what to say in the heat of the moment. You'll be too tired or stressed to be patient. And all of that is okay. You are a (lovely and fallible) human being. Those long-term goals and hopes are still your foundation, reminding you of the destination.

This is the primary reason positive parenting starts with us. Our children will continue to react in ways we can't expect. Remember that time your toddler had a tantrum because you pulled the drain of the bathtub when it was *his* turn? Or the day your tween decided it was mortifying when you sang along to a song when literally the day before, it had been fine? We just can't anticipate what they will do. But we can keep coming back to recognizing what's happening at this moment and doing our best to choose our response. Luckily, our kids will give us plenty of opportunities to try again (whether we want them or not).

up with what social media would have you do, what your neighbor across the street does, or what that mother in the PTA—who is somehow never late—is doing, and it hurts to try. You don't have to. If nothing else, letting go of that self-comparison is a huge step toward self-care.

MODELING REGULATION, OR WHEN I LOSE MY $%@$, I'M A GREAT TEACHER, NOT A BAD PARENT

Believe it or not, one of the best things you can do for your children's emotional well-being is to show them that you aren't perfect. You make mistakes, don't always know what you're doing, and, just like them, sometimes you feel frustrated, angry, or sad. This gives them permission to feel their own feelings and it lets them see that everyone does, in fact, make mistakes. Of course, it's what you do with those feelings and those mistakes that makes all the difference. Watching you self-regulate models that behavior for them, so when they come up against their own frustrations, big emotions, and mistakes, they will be less likely to beat themselves up and more likely to have and use helpful tools. Our parental meltdowns actually help them build emotional regulation tools and vocabulary as well as normalize that all emotions are valid. So, the next time you lose your $%@$ (as I did right before I wrote this) you can remind yourself that you don't have to feel guilty about it. You're a great teacher, not a bad parent!

Patterns and Expectations

As part of developing mindful awareness, it's helpful to pay attention to any patterns and expectations that might influence your parenting.

PATTERNS

Our behavior is shaped by our conditioning. Sometimes this is obvious. If you were bitten by a dog, you are more likely to fear dogs, less likely to have one, and less likely to encourage your children to pet dogs you pass on the sidewalk. When it comes to parenting, how we were treated as children affects how we treat our children.

In order to parent with conscious awareness, it's helpful to identify patterns that might have an impact on how we react. When we are stressed, we often regress and get caught in old patterns that may or may not be helpful. You might take a moment now to reflect on how your own parents, guardians, teachers, or authority figures responded to you. How might your childhood impact how you parent?

_____

_____

_____

_____

_____

Patterns Exercise Continued on next page.

Patterns Exercise Continued from previous page.

_____

_____

_____

_____

_____

_____

_____

_____

_____

_____

_____

_____

_____

_____

_____

_____

_____

_____

Sometimes the messages were overt. One teen with whom I worked shared that she never lets herself cry because when she was a child, she was told crying made her look ugly. That's a damaging message to internalize, one likely to have a long-lasting impact. Other messages are more subtle. Our tendencies toward things like perfectionism and guilt might be nature and/or nurture.

Looking at our patterns isn't about blaming or getting caught up in some psychoanalytic "my parents made me do it" analysis. It's actually not about *why* the pattern is there at all. That might be a key part of your journey, but it's peripheral to this particular exercise. The idea is that in order to be able to respond to our children the way we want in any given moment, it's helpful to acknowledge what might be getting in our way. We might ultimately decide to change the patterns one day, but we can't change anything without first being able to acknowledge it.

EXPECTATIONS

The other inquiry you might find helpful is to consider any previously unexplored expectations you have of your children (and also of yourself). You're likely aware of many expectations and assumptions, but chances are a lot of them are lurking underneath the surface. Are you expecting perfect listening or obedience? Quiet? To remember every birthday or key date?

This can be a helpful exercise to do in a heated moment. A lot of the time we end up yelling at or losing it with our children because our expectations are not being met. When we show up for pickup at school after a busy day at work and they aren't ready or are having their own tough day, it can throw us off guard or upset us because it just wasn't what we expected. We just want to get home and now we have to deal with this?!

The problem with expectations is they tend to rob us of the chance to be okay with what's happening at that moment. Think about how many of the expectations you have for yourself that are actually obstacles to your well-being. If I expect myself to have energy all the time, I'm going to get pretty frustrated when I'm constantly tired. If we only focus on how we *should* be, then we never get to be satisfied with who we actually are. And the same goes for our kids. We want to be present for them as they are, rather than getting stuck in unconscious assumptions or expectations.

You're still allowed to have expectations. The idea is to be able to see those expectations so you can choose which you want to focus on, which are connected to your long-term goals, and which might be obstacles.

Not Taking Things Personally

When my daughter was about 18 months old, she went through a protracted phase where she didn't want anything to do with me whenever my husband was around. When she needed comforting, I'd rush to pick her up, but she only wanted her dad. When she wanted to play, she'd turn to him first. I knew it wasn't personal. I knew her little 18-month-old brain wasn't making logical decisions. But after what felt like the billionth time, it was really hard not to take it personally. It wasn't deliberate, but still, my feelings were hurt and I felt like a bad mother.

When our children don't like what we cook, don't want to take the lessons we sign them up for, lash out at us, prefer the company of their friends, or even when they say "I hate you," very rarely is it personal. It's some combination of their stage of development, their navigation of their own identities, and their nervous systems responding to what's happening. That doesn't mean we should ignore their anger or behavior but that we should see them for what they are. When our kids hit their siblings, fail a class, or don't want to spend any time with us, our automatic reaction might be, *I'm a terrible parent*, accompanied by anger. It takes a ton of practice to be able to let those automatic reactions go, to replace *I'm a terrible parent* with *There's something up with my child that is making her feel big feelings and lash out.* The yelling and the fights often come from our automatic reactions rather than from what's actually true in the moment. One of the best gifts we can give ourselves is to acknowledge those reactions and give ourselves some compassion as we make the effort not to take things personally.

Conclusion

The mindful awareness and deliberate responses of positive parenting start with us. In fact, it's really an approach about us far more than it is about them. It's primarily about how we respond to any given moment with our children. Their behavior and actions are not in our control, anyway. But although it starts with us, it's vital to remember that it's not about us. Their behavior is just what's happening at that moment in their nervous systems. They aren't doing it to piss us off. Usually, when we get angry it's because whatever they are doing is contrary to what we expected or can handle at that moment.

That means that the first thing we need to do when connecting with our children is to connect to ourselves: our own bodies, nervous systems, expectations, and feelings in the present moment; to know that it's okay to feel however we feel. We want to remember that it's okay when we react automatically (because that's what people naturally do). Then we can take a breath and choose how we want to respond next. We are modeling these skills for them and being more present for them, but ultimately, self-care is something we need for ourselves.

It's easy to talk about taking a breath before choosing how to respond to our children, but it's really hard to remember to do it in a heated moment. One of the reasons it's so challenging is that we've trained ourselves to react quickly and often harshly when something goes amiss. Not just with them, but also with ourselves. When we make a mistake at work, when we get a speeding ticket, or when we forget an important date, our usual reaction is to beat ourselves up. Consider how you talk to yourself when you're down. You probably berate yourself pretty harshly. Very few of us would ever talk to anyone else as cruelly as we talk to ourselves.

One of the best ways to take care of ourselves is to see what's happening in this moment and respond with kindness.

1. Whatever is going on, take a few deep breaths. See if you can feel your breath in your body and your feet on the ground.
2. Letting your breathing be natural, take a few more moments to notice how you feel.

3. You can use the exercises in this chapter to help you see what's happening beneath any thoughts and to give your emotions a name.
4. Whatever you are noticing, try to add "and it's okay" to the phrase. *I made a mistake ... and it's okay. I'm feeling angry ... and it's okay. My mind is racing ... and it's okay.*
5. You don't have to make any thought, feeling, or sensation go away. You don't have to make anything happen at all. Just focus on allowing yourself to notice this moment and let it be okay just as it is.

It's really helpful to practice this when things aren't heated, so you can have those skills when you really need them in the moment. You can also do this throughout your day to promote a sense of equanimity with everything that happens on a daily basis.

This exercise helps us remember that we can't change what's happening without first acknowledging it, and that beating ourselves up for feeling or thinking something only makes us feel worse.

CHAPTER 4

Build a Foundation for Success

Helicopter, tiger, attachment, free range, vegan, hybrid . . . there are so many different ways to try to get your kid to put their shoes on in the morning. If I consider all the ways I've tried to get my daughter's cooperation, they include but are not limited to yelling, pleading (I'm really not proud of that one), joking, cajoling, pretending to be Captain Underpants, the "I have no idea why this works but I'm going to be so sad when it stops," 5-4-3-2-1 countdown, challenging her to races to see who can get their shoes on the fastest, singing my requests, offering points for Gryffindor, asking her if something was bothering her first, writing it in a note, using her stuffed animals to give the message, and going to another room for a bit so I could collect myself enough to try again.

And yet it seems like the demands of parenting are out-pacing all the tactics and resources. Studies show that we spend more time engaged in the act of parenting than any other generation before us. It's no wonder we're all exhausted. We are spending more time parenting but still lack the tools to know what the heck we're doing. Add in economic and environmental uncertainty and it's a perfect storm of stress.

This chapter hopes to remedy some of that by going back to the basics and offering tools to make positive parenting work for you by building on the work you've explored in previous chapters. Our long-term goals are always at the heart of this approach. Now, we explore what comes next.

Creating the Container

In my work training educators to teach their students mindfulness, we spend a lot of time talking about "creating a container." It's our shorthand for making a place where students feel safe, respected, and heard; it is a place where they can be themselves and try new things. It's similar to the space we are trying to create at home.

A container or safe space has two main parts: warmth and structure. We create firm expectations, boundaries, and rules and infuse them with caring, love, and connection.

SUGGESTIONS FOR CREATING A SAFE SPACE

No one can tell you exactly what this looks like in your own home, and it will change depending on the temperament, age, and needs of your child. Still, most safe spaces share similar traits and strategies.

Setting clear expectations and consequences: Have you ever had someone get angry at you because you failed to do something they expected, even though they never told you what it was or how to do it? One of the most supportive things we can do as parents is to be clear about our expectations and the consequences when those expectations are not met. This helps our children feel safe and supported because the expectations and rules aren't arbitrary; they are in place for the safety and well-being of the whole family.

Making sure rules and their reasons are clear: Rules should be understandable (appropriate to the child's age and level of development), doable, and specific. We can help our children succeed much more easily when we say, "The jacket belongs in the closet" rather than "Clean up this mess" or "Why is this place such a pigsty?" Explaining the reasons for the rules gives children the knowledge to follow through and understand why. This helps them comprehend the larger picture so that they can make sense of their world and feel secure in it. It also promotes critical thinking and discussion because we are giving them the opportunity to understand and to ask questions.

Trusting them/building respect: Positive parenting is about cultivating the tools children need to thrive. We don't want to be authoritarian and tell them exactly what to do *because we said so*. If we want them to feel safe, loved, and secure, we need to trust them and build mutual respect. So, we give them age-appropriate responsibilities and trust that they will follow through. We explain the rationale or relevance behind an action or direction. We don't jump in the moment something goes awry but instead give them the chance to try things on their own. We communicate clearly and listen openly.

Being consistent: It's not enough simply to know the expectations and consequences; children need to be able to trust and count on them. Inconsistency creates uncertainty and doubt. Not only will kids try (harder) to push the boundaries, but they won't feel safe enough to make mistakes or try new things, too.

Letting them fall and fail: We all want what's best for our children and we hate to see them in pain. But coddling them actually does the opposite of what we intend; overprotection stifles rather than frees. We need to give them room to fall down and make mistakes. One of the best pieces of advice that I got as a new mother was to wait. When the baby starts crying, just wait a moment to see if she can soothe herself before swooping in. When she falls, wait; give her an opportunity to pick herself back up. We want to let our children figure things out for themselves (as long as it's safe, of course). We want them to know that we will love them no matter what, that everyone makes mistakes, and that mistakes are how we learn. We are giving them permission to fail, which means they feel safe enough to do so.

Loving and offering warmth: Love and warmth manifest in many different ways. It might be spending time together, providing physical affection, verbal connection, believing in them, encouraging them, playing together, and/or sharing time and energy. We are offering them emotional security through our presence, affection, listening, and connection.

Being sensitive and empathic: Just as with love and warmth, children's connection and security comes from knowing that we are there for them just as they are. This means we need to be aware of what they are experiencing and sensitive to what it's like to be a kid, knowing that each of our kids will respond differently, with different needs at different times.

Taking responsibility for ourselves: There is a lot about our own emotions and thoughts that we can't control. Sometimes it's impossible to be truly consistent when we are going through something ourselves. This is where it's essential to regulate our own nervous systems and model honesty, responsibility, and connection. When we make mistakes (which of course we will), our children can expect that we will recognize them, make amends, and communicate. In this case, consistency comes in the form of how we respond to mistakes, not necessarily avoiding mistakes or emotions altogether.

Being a team: Listening and collaborating are fundamental to creating a safe space. When our children are very small, we do most of the "work" ourselves. But as they grow up, we want to make sure they know they are a part of a team that together tackles challenges, solves problems, and helps each other. We want to hear and value our children's ideas, input, and suggestions. We still set the rules, but we all create a safe, loving, communicative environment.

Believing in them: This one also sounds obvious, perhaps. Maybe you read the same advice as a new parent that I did, something about how if you believe your child can sleep well, she will. If you believe she can't, she won't. I have no ability to measure if my beliefs helped my kid be the amazing sleeper she is, but I do know they helped foster an environment where believing in her was a given. As pediatrician and professor of pediatrics Kenneth Ginsburg puts it: "Youngsters live up or down to their parents' expectations."

Letting go of outcomes: There's only so much we can control. We set up the container in a way that lets our children feel safe and then we have to let go of what happens next. This is important not just because we can't control what happens but also so our children can explore their own agency within this safe space. If we try to force a particular way of being or specific outcomes, they can't be free to discover their own ways.

CREATING CONSISTENCY

I learned the importance of consistency firsthand with my baby daughter's sleep schedule. It was very firmly set, and I was adamant about sticking to it because it worked. She needed sleep, we both needed consistency, and we both thrived. But the schedule was about her being in her crib. I couldn't force her to go to sleep. All I could do was to set the conditions.

The same thing applies now. Her bedtime is firm. We read a story and then we say goodnight. Between then and her lights-out time, she is allowed to do what she wants as long as she doesn't leave the bed. Does it work all the time? Of course not. (Did I mention that she once convinced a babysitter to provide fresh fruit after bedtime?) But we are clear and firm that the rules do not change and that they are for her health and well-being since she needs so many hours of sleep to feel good.

Validating feelings: We want our children to know it's okay to feel however they feel. This doesn't mean all actions are acceptable but that all emotions are valid. Part of self-regulation and long-term well-being for them and us comes from seeing and befriending emotions so we can all choose how to respond to them.

Letting go of distraction: As one of my favorite characters, Ron Swanson from *Parks and Recreation,* would say, "Don't half-ass two things. Whole-ass one thing." We want our children to know that we are there for them and that they can trust us. We demonstrate this through our attention. It doesn't mean we have to give them all our focus. We just have to do our best to focus on one thing at a time.

Communicating clearly and openly: Communication is integral to this approach and we will cover it more below. The basic idea is that our children know that they can speak freely without recrimination and that we will listen openly with as little judgment as possible.

A general guideline is that parenting is a bit like tuning a violin or guitar. If it's too tight, the strings will break. Too loose and there's not enough tension for anything to work. The goal is finding what fits for you and your family and then revising whenever necessary.

Communication

When my daughter wants to share information, she often asks, "Can I tell you something?" It's one of my favorite habits because then I get to respond, "You can always tell me anything." Whether she's telling me about her joys and fears, how she's part cheetah and part vampire, or plans for her birthday party, my intention is the same: to let her know that I am always there for her.

Communication is a top priority in our house. We tell our daughter we will always love her, no matter what. We tell her when we are getting frustrated. We talk about everything. I tell her she can ask me any question; I won't always have the answer, but she and I can find it together. All of this promotes a feeling of security and connection.

But this makes it sound easy. True communication isn't always easy or natural. It takes work and practice, because what's easy is getting caught up in thoughts or distracted by automatic judgments or other things going on.

INTENTION AND CONNECTION

Our intentions are a key foundation for good communication. Setting the intention to care first and foremost, to be open to what the other person is sharing and experiencing, and to be curious but nonjudgmental allows for true listening and connecting. We often come into a conversation with a specific, narrow agenda or distracted by other things, which tends to close us off to a real exchange.

As with any other skill, good communication takes practice. This doesn't mean rehearsing what you're going to say but practicing noticing your intentions as you begin a conversation and working to be present, mindfully and without judgment. You can do this with your children but also with your partner, coworkers, friends, or other family members. Notice if you've decided how the conversation is going to go before you start. Practice taking a deep breath before you speak and, while the other person is speaking, see if you can be open to what this person might offer (even if you disagree). Notice what it's like to be curious and to care about connecting with this person, in whatever way is appropriate. Practice is vital because we are trying to build new habits, and when we are tired or stressed, we tend to fall back into our old, not always helpful patterns.

With positive parenting, we want to prioritize connection first and foremost. This isn't just about getting children to do something or having our say. *How* we say something often matters more than what we say. This approach goes back to the collective nervous system we talked about in chapter 3. If we come at a conversation agitated, stressed, and distracted, our children will feel and feed off that and will be less likely to feel connected to us. If we are focused on being in the present moment with kindness and curiosity, they will feel heard.

Not every conversation needs to be a deep, life-changing discussion. You can have meaningful conversations when you pick the kids up from school or when you are asking them if they brushed their teeth. It's about choosing to connect first.

LISTENING

Just like us, children want to be heard. And although we want to be good listeners, life often gets in the way. Think about how often your child gets interrupted. It's probably a lot. When we interrupt them, we give them the message that what they have to say isn't important. Admittedly, your four-year-old's treatise on dinosaurs might not be the most scintillating thing you've heard. But again, this is about the long term. We want them to know that we care and their voices matter.

This isn't to say that you can never interrupt. If your child is anything like mine, you might have to interrupt otherwise you won't get a word in at all. We just want to be clear about the intention to listen and be present for what they have to say.

Likewise, think about how many times we say things like, "You can't possibly be hungry; you just ate," or "Why are you so tired? You had a good night's sleep," or "But you love your gymnastics class." It's totally natural to react this way, but once we do so, we've not only closed ourselves off to really hearing what's going on, but we might also be leading our children to doubt that we trust them, making it less likely that they will continue to be open and honest with us about how they are feeling.

To foster trust, build more connection, and promote the healthy development of our children, it's important to seek to understand their needs and their position. We need to listen openly and with the intention of closeness, without preparing a response in advance.

We don't have to agree with or even like what they say. But it makes a world of difference to be open to what they are feeling and going through and to let them know we care. When they say something that gets our blood boiling or makes us concerned, we have the opportunity to be aware of those reactions, to check our nervous systems, and then to communicate openly back to them: "I hear you saying that you want to ___. That makes me feel nervous. Can we talk about it some more?"

You might consider scheduling a monthly family meeting or event that lets everyone share openly. Conversations over the dishes are good, but it's useful to supplement them with time devoted to communicating. This also lets children know there is always a space for them to share. And yes, if you have older kids, this suggestion might engender serious eye rolling, but that's mostly unavoidable at this point so you might as well go for it anyway.

TALKING

Even with our best intentions, it can be helpful to have specific techniques for communicating. Our approach in this book is based on nonviolent communication (also known as compassionate communication). Pioneered by Marshall Rosenberg, it's an approach that offers specific strategies to build on the innate human capacities for compassion and empathy.

Generally, it's more supportive to express what's going on in terms of what you see and how it makes you feel rather than what the other person is doing or automatic reactions. "You are so frustrating" can shut down the conversation a lot faster than "I feel very frustrated right now."

This approach follows four main components, which both the speaker and the empathic listener use.

1. **Observations:** saying/receiving what you see, feel, hear, remember, imagine as objectively and nonjudgmentally as possible

2. **Feelings:** saying/receiving what you are feeling, expressing emotions

3. **Needs:** sharing/receiving empathically what needs are not being met

4. **Requests:** offering/hearing concrete ideas that would help meet your needs

We can use the ubiquitous "clean your room" argument to illustrate what this might look like.

Scenario one:

> *After a stressful day, you see your child's room. It's filthy. You immediately get angry. This is the millionth time this has happened. You begin yelling, "I've asked you a million times to clean your room. It's disgusting! You never listen. Why can't you just do what I ask for once?"*

Now, imagine the child's reaction. Most of us can understand the parent's perspective, but these statements are full of judgments, blaming, and personal criticism. The child will likely feel attacked and possibly lash out in retaliation, leading to more arguing and less connection (and less room cleaning). This method of communication is more about punishment and autopilot than discipline and conscious response.

Scenario two:

> *After a stressful day, you see your child's room. It's filthy. You immediately get angry. This is the millionth time this has happened. You want to start yelling. You stop yourself and take a breath (or a longer break) to decide how to deal with this situation before responding with: "I see there are clothes all over the floor and the bed isn't made. I'm feeling really frustrated. I've asked you to clean it many times. It seems you don't respect the rules of the house that are really important to me. Can you please clean everything up before dinner?"*

You can imagine the child's reaction here, too. Besides looking at you like you've grown a second head because you're being weird, this will make them pause. You aren't attacking or blaming. You are presenting the situation in a way that everyone can relate to and you're giving them an opportunity to respond.

Obviously, how you apply this will vary widely depending on the situation and the age of your children. Yet even with a toddler you can say, "I'm seeing dirty hands. That can lead to germs. Let's go wash our hands together."

And of course, nothing is magic. Communicating more effectively does not mean your child's room will stay clean, that he or she will listen, or that all yelling will cease. It's helpful to practice compassionate communication, but this is still a child's room (or curfew, or homework, or any of the other challenges we face) that we are talking about: They are basically rites of passage and aren't going away any time soon. But even if your house stays messy, you've opened up the path to greater respect, trust, and listening through more open, compassionate communication.

CONVERSATION TRAPS

Most of us regularly fall into certain unhelpful traps in conversations. The goal here isn't to beat ourselves up about them but to do our best to see when we fall into these traps, forgive ourselves, and then choose an approach that promotes more give-and-take. Here are some of the more common pitfalls:

- **Blaming the other person or ourselves:** Even if someone *is* at fault, we want to encourage taking responsibility rather than casting blame.

- **Global judgments:** It's better to stay specific than to make overarching statements about ourselves or others.

- **Black-and-white statements:** There's almost always an exception to the rule. "Always" and "never" statements cut off chances for growth and change and tend to make others defensive.

- **Unhelpful listening:** This includes not listening at all but also rushing in to give advice without being asked, offering pity rather than empathy, one-upping the other person with our own story, or when a conversation turns into an interrogation.

OTHER HELPFUL COMMUNICATION HINTS

Use do statements instead of don'ts: "Hold the cup with two hands" is a lot easier to follow than "Don't spill." It's really hard for anyone to comply with a "don't" statement because it's not clear what should be done instead. To support our children better, it's best to use positively framed statements.

Talking to them directly: Parents often talk to their partners or other adults *about* the children rather than talking *to* the children themselves. Part of empowering our children means trusting their (age-appropriate) maturity and responsibility. Making eye contact and getting down to their level (for little ones) is crucial.

Use fewer words: Parents tend to over-explain and lecture when simply pointing something out is more effective. "I see dirty clothes on the floor" has more impact than

"Your clothes are on the floor again. I've told you a hundred times that you have to pick up your clothes. You need to take more responsibility for yourself, etc., etc."

Ask questions: Instead of lecturing, which they tune out anyway, get them involved. Ask your children, "How can we solve this?"

Watch out for thoughts masquerading as feelings: "I feel ignored" may be true but it isn't actually a feeling. It's a judgment based on the situation, one that can lead to blaming. The feeling in this case might be hurt or sad: "I feel sad because we didn't spend time together this week." Naming feelings normalizes all feelings as valid and underscores that it's okay to share how we are feeling without needing anyone else to fix or solve it.

USING COMMUNICATION TO FOSTER A GROWTH MINDSET

Growth and fixed mindsets refer to our underlying, though not unalterable, beliefs about learning. They often determine how we handle failure. Fixed mindset individuals (those who believe that intelligence or talent is mostly static) are more likely to take setbacks or failure with great disappointment and have difficulty rebounding. Growth mindset individuals believe their intelligence and talents could grow with effort and are able to rebound from setbacks much more easily. Chances are one of your long-term goals for your children is for them to have a growth mindset: to focus on learning and effort more than outcome, to see failure as an opportunity for growth, and to try new approaches in order to have a different result.

One of the primary tactics for promoting a growth mindset is changing how we use praise. The basic ideas are that we want to keep praise specific, seek to foster dialogue, and focus on effort and learning rather than traits or innate qualities.

Research shows that children whose intelligence is praised can actually suffer because they come to believe their intelligence is a fixed trait. Then failure or poor showing becomes a matter of their fundamental abilities—which can't be changed in a fixed mindset—rather than their efforts and strategies, which always have room for growth.

Here are some strategies for fostering growth mindsets in children:

Be specific and authentic: Instead of saying, "Good job," you might say, "You worked so hard mastering that new move" or "I loved how you enjoyed yourself on stage."

Describe/engender dialogue: Instead of "Great painting" or "You're such a good artist," you might say, "I see you chose a lot of blue for this painting. Can you tell me more about it?" Or ask them what they are most proud of in their painting or game.

Praise effort, learning, or process instead of traits: Instead of "You're so smart," you might say, "You've done such a great job working so hard at this assignment" or "I can tell you've been trying something new." Praising process cultivates motivation whereas praising traits actually weakens it.

Focus on the behavior when expressing frustration: We want to be clear that we love our children no matter what and that we understand that mistakes happen. Therefore, it's important to express frustration or disappointment with the situation or the behavior, not them. For example, "I'm frustrated with this messy room" rather than "Why are you such a slob?"

Respond to setbacks with realism and encouragement for future learning: It's much more helpful to say "Let's talk about what you've tried and what you can do next" instead of "Great effort, you tried your best." Adding "yet" to a statement can also be very helpful. When fixed mindset–inclined children say, "I can't do it. I'm no good at this," we can help them appreciate that they're always learning. So "I can't do it" becomes "I can't do it yet." We want them to see that flourishing actually comes from growing and trying new things rather than always getting something right. "I'm no good at this" becomes "I can learn new ways of approaching it."

Focusing on communication is integral to positive parenting. It's about finding common ground through compassion and communicating in a way that lets everyone feel heard and respected while working toward a course of action that fits the individuals and the situation. And it uses the skills we've been exploring already: mindful awareness, patience, responding rather than reacting, and using each moment as an opportunity for growth and connection.

How Brain Science Helps
with Perspective

A while back, I had an experience that really opened my eyes to the impact of checking my assumptions before making judgments. I was in line at the grocery store with only one person ahead of me, and it was taking *forever*. I was getting increasingly agitated and caught up in the thoughts running through my mind: *Why is this taking so long? Don't people have any respect for someone else's time? I'm going to be late.* Then I noticed that the person in front of me had severe physical challenges. He was having incredible trouble unloading each item from his cart. It was an immense task to take out his wallet. From that moment, everything changed. Instead of being frustrated, I felt compassionate toward him and embarrassed by my own reaction. I sheepishly realized that I had interpreted the situation solely on my very limited perspective. This person was doing the best he could. If he could have done better, he would have.

It's the same with our kids. If we know that our toddlers can't help having the tantrum, it doesn't make the screaming any quieter, but it might help us keep things in perspective. If we know that teenagers often can't help making poor decisions, it might change how we respond.

So, guess what are totally natural, generally unavoidable, and to-be-expected parts of the stages of development of your child's brain?

The answer is pretty much all those behaviors that drive you crazy. Your two-year-old throwing a tantrum because you wouldn't let her put rocks up her nose? Your fifteen-year-old being overly swayed by his friends? Your teenager staying up too late and then complaining about being tired in the morning? All relatively predictable.

When your children were babies, you knew they weren't crying or keeping you awake on purpose; they simply couldn't behave differently. It's so much harder to know what's really going on with the same certainty as they grow up because, unless you happen to have a background in child psychology and developmental neuroscience, you probably haven't been given the necessary information. And although there's a ton of accessible data on milestones by age, there isn't a lot of detail on *why* those milestones occur. Consider this section an attempt to fill in that gap so you can see what's really happening with your kids when they are (inadvertently) driving you crazy.

WHAT'S HAPPENING IN MY CHILD'S BRAIN

Toddler

The brain of a three-year-old has reached 80 percent of its adult size but is still very much in development. In the toddler's brain, everything is pretty much fight or flight. Their brain function is centered on the limbic system (the part of the brain that's all about emotional responses.) The limbic system's key action is to sound an alarm when it feels a threat, and it's important to know that neither the alarm nor the threat need to correspond to reality. That's why your toddler has a tantrum because you put the carrots too close to the chicken.

This is even more challenging for toddlers because they don't have any previously learned reference points, so anything new can become a cause for alarm. That's why cutting their sandwich the wrong way causes howls as if they are in physical pain. We've unknowingly violated their safety because we've done something different.

Furthermore, psychologist Philip Zelazo explains that three-year-olds lack the ability to be flexible about rules, which is why they can't adapt and why new rules or conflicting instructions are so upsetting. Consistency and clarity of rules can be a parent's best friend.

From a developmental perspective, co-regulation is a parent's primary process in these early years. We are continually helping our children manage their own nervous system arousal (the fight-or-flight response). As we help them return to a state of deactivation when they repeatedly experience emotional outbursts and become upset, we promote a sense of trust, security, and connection.

Preschooler

The neurological processing in the preschooler's brain is twice as busy as that of a 20-year-old and perhaps three times busier than an adult's. This might explain why children five and under can't really focus on multiple things. That's also why it's helpful to give instructions slowly, one at a time. Their immature prefrontal cortex (the part of the brain responsible for executive function) makes it difficult for them to stop what they're doing and switch tasks. This is why it can be helpful to incorporate visual tools, such as a picture checklist they can follow.

Although their cognitive abilities are greater than that of the toddler, they actually might melt down more often and more dramatically precisely because they start to have a sense of how the world works. Anything they don't expect can lead to a terrific tantrum because it has overturned their understanding of how things are and how they're supposed to be.

It's helpful at this age to make sure children have enough downtime. There is so much going on in their brains and their worlds that they can get overstimulated rather quickly. Building in quiet time also helps them develop the skills to take care of themselves later on.

Grade School Age

As our children enter elementary school, their brain development accelerates, as does their desire to be independent and to form social connections with friends. These years are full of changes and growth but are often given less attention than the years that come before and after because the changes are less dramatic.

Children at this age think largely in concrete terms. Although their grasp of the abstract will improve as these years progress, in order for something to be understood it needs to be experienced, largely with the senses. From ages five to nine, children are more flexible and adaptable. As their brains are increasingly refined through a process called synaptic pruning (a bit like weeding in the garden), their neural pathways become stronger and parts that aren't used are discarded.

It is still hard for older elementary children at this stage to filter out unrelated or extraneous information during learning, so keeping distractions to a minimum and focusing on clear instructions can be helpful. In addition, the thickening of the part of the brain that supports planning, organizing, strategizing, and paying attention peaks at age 11 to 12 for boys and earlier for girls. As a result, children get better at self-regulation and their emotional outbursts might decrease while their tendency for abstract thought will increase.

While all this is taking place, parents still tend to over-estimate the abilities of grade school children to make good decisions. Children at this age and stage need us to guide and nurture them while giving them plenty of opportunities to exercise their independence.

Adolescence

Al Bernstein once said, "Adolescence is a period of rapid changes. Between the ages of 12 and 17, for example, parents age as much as 20 years." Scientists used to think that the teenage brain was just a less mature adult brain, functioning in largely the same way. We now know that the differences are profound. Teenagers aren't just younger adults; their brains function in dramatically different ways. Whereas the adult's thought processes are largely ruled by the prefrontal cortex (the cognitive center of the brain responsible for fear modulation, emotional regulation, empathy, considering con-sequences, and decision making), the teen's brain is ruled by the emotional, reactive amygdala. This makes sense when we consider that our brains don't finish developing until age 24 or 25 and the last part to develop fully is the prefrontal cortex. Teens don't have the full capacities of their rational brains, but their emotional centers are at their peak. This can explain why teens have difficulty with long-term problem solving and thinking and are less likely to consider consequences before they act.

So when your teen doesn't have a good reason for why he did something, or you wonder what on earth he was thinking, it's actually because his brain wasn't thinking as much as it was feeling.

The wiring of your teen's brain and how efficient it is at relaying messages is still largely in development, too. Although the gray matter of the brain (neurons that form the basic unit of the nervous system responsible for receiving and relaying signals) is largely developed by age six, the white matter (the wiring between the cells) doesn't finish developing until the mid-20s. In fact, it's only 80 percent developed by age 18. At the same time, teen brains are undergoing a process called myelination, which is a type of insulation for those connections, allowing signals to travel faster and more efficiently.

So not only is the prefrontal cortex underdeveloped, but the wiring and the insulation to it are under construction. It's no wonder teens have a harder time making good decisions and considering the consequences of their actions.

Furthermore, teens' limbic systems are hypersensitive to the rewarding feeling of risk taking. Add hormones, peer pressure, and the need to express their individuality into the mix and you have a neurological cocktail for risky behaviors.

Studies show that teens have trouble multitasking as well as adults do. Their brains are still sorting out the ability for strategic, higher-order thinking.

For tweens and early teens, the focus on identity development helps explain why they are so self-obsessed. They are literally trying to figure out who they are. And it's true that teens need a different sleep cycle than they are used to. Sleep mechanisms in teens really are different. They actually aren't wired to be able to wake up early.

This means that although your teenagers might be driving you crazy, they aren't doing so on purpose. And although they are keen to prove their independence, they also need you. They need to be able to trust you and use you as a resource until their rational brains catch up. Professor of neurology and senior neurologist Frances Jensen encourages parents to act as a surrogate prefrontal cortex for their teens, thinking for them until their own brains are ready for the job.

Teens still have to take responsibility, but it's not totally their fault that they do reckless things. And if this all sounds like fighting a losing battle, it might be heartening to know that positive parenting practices like the ones in this book have been shown to predict fewer risky behaviors among adolescents.

Just Be with Them

The last piece in creating the foundation of positive parenting is quite simple, though admittedly not always easy: Just be with them. Spend time together. It doesn't have to be fancy or momentous. Listen to the music they like, throw a ball, or go for a walk. Even time spent in the car counts. This is similar to the advice parents or guardians get about the importance of date nights. Just as we need special time with our partners that's removed from everyday life, so do our children. One of the best things we can do for our relationships with our children is to spend time with them, with no agenda or plan other than to be together.

Conclusion

The foundation of positive parenting is the safe space we create in our homes. We are building trust, setting expectations, providing warmth and boundaries, and attuning to their needs and feelings. Communication helps us create this space, where children feel safe, heard, respected, and loved, a space where they can thrive and build helpful skills and qualities for their futures.

Understanding child and adolescent brain development helps us put behavior into context. If we can understand that those frustrating actions aren't done on purpose and are a normal part of childhood development, we are more likely to be able to keep things in perspective and help our children manage all these changes together.

SELF-CARE BREAK: Dear You/Love, Me

For this moment of self-care, write yourself a note or a letter, something you can come back to when you're really down, need some support, or are having a particularly hard time. What would you really want or need to hear when you are feeling lost? You might consider what your best friend, partner, or loved one would tell you when you're struggling, probably something about how you're doing great, how you've been through tough times before, or how you are incredibly strong even if you sometimes forget it.

You can do this any way you like, though you might consider beginning with "Dear You" and ending with "Love, Me." Write this letter for yourself and keep it somewhere so when you need your own support, you will have it.

Doing this as a family is a great option, too. You don't have to read each other's letters (though that can be quite poignant). It's just a reminder to each of us that we can pause and take care of ourselves and trust that we have wisdom and compassion within each of us, even if we lose sight of it a lot of the time.

CHAPTER 5

Putting Ideas into Practice

So far, we've covered the building blocks of positive parenting: identifying our goals and obstacles, considering why discipline fits and punishment doesn't, checking our own nervous systems and expectations, creating a container, communicating clearly, and understanding what might be going on in our kids' brains. Now it's time to put all that together as we explore steps to follow and supportive tools to use in the real world.

Emotional Regulation

What do you actually do when your toddler throws a tantrum in public, your tween refuses to leave their room until you get them a phone, or your children are hitting each other?

The truth is that although the scenarios will change, our approach to them follows a similar pattern. It looks something like this:

Thing happens.

1. First, pause and regulate your own nervous system (unless there is immediate danger).

2. Connect before trying to fix, solve, or discipline.

3. Before, during, and after connecting, consider what's really going on.

4. Help them self-regulate.

5. Take their perspective. Listen and let go of the script.

6. Acknowledge what's happening. Validate feelings.

7. When the time is right, problem solve together.

8. Use discipline tools and consequences that fit.

Your experience will likely not follow this order exactly. You will be helping them self-regulate throughout. You'll validate feelings as you take their perspective and consider what's really happening. Use this pattern as a supportive guide rather than an instruction manual.

Now that we have the steps, let's break them down into more detail.

STEP ONE: Oxygen Mask On

You get that dreaded call to come get your child from school, your son comes home with a black eye, or you discover that your daughter has been bullying a classmate. Each scenario causes your heart to race, puts your nerves on edge, and makes you feel panicked and/or angry. The last thing you want to do is pause and breathe—you want to plunge in and fix the situation as fast as possible. But as we've already explored, the first step in helping our children is supporting ourselves, connecting to what's happening in our own bodies, minds, and hearts. We are actually more supportive when we are (relatively) collected and when we give our children a moment to help themselves first, and that's our goal. We are just the guides. So, while we do the necessary step of self-regulation, we also give them the opportunity to take charge of their own needs in the situation.

We are also modeling self-regulation for them. As psychologist Louis Cozolino puts it: "While it might feel impossible to just let your furious teenager rail and yell at you, modelling self-regulation is actually a gift, not only for the modelling of regulation and not escalating but for providing that safe space for them to feel however they feel."

Checking your own system is often about letting go of the thoughts running through your mind and focusing on the feelings in your body, especially the feelings of breathing. Taking a deep breath is actually a signal to your nervous system that you are safe (even if everything still feels crazy) and it helps you calm down so you can be present for your child.

STEP TWO: Connect

Take a moment to recall an argument or disagreement with a loved one. What happens when you're still fuming and they try to explain their position or want to talk it through? Usually we can't hear them at all, it makes us more enraged, or we just don't have the ability to stop and listen. Our emotions hijack our rationality.

In the last fifteen years, researchers have found that, contrary to the conventionally held view in neuroscience, all brain signals don't have to go through the neocortex (the thinking, rational part of the brain). Some, in fact, go almost straight to the emotional, reactive amygdala, which processes them before they even make it to the more rational parts of the brain. This is one reason why we react emotionally before we can think things through logically.

When the amygdala is triggered, the prefrontal cortex is impaired. That means that even if the rational part gets the signal first, once the emotional, reactive part fires, it's difficult to get our rational selves back online. That's why we often need a moment (or several) to calm down before being ready to hash it out.

This hijacking of rationality is even more true for children because, as noted, their rational brains won't be fully developed until their mid-20s, but their emotional brains are already raring to go. If we try to solve, fix, or often even address the problem while our children are upset, we will likely fuel their emotions and exacerbate what's happening, which is quite the opposite of our intentions. Also, when they are in fight-or-flight mode, their brains are almost entirely focused on the threat and they can't really hear us. They won't be able to address anything until their nervous systems find balance again. Not only that, but any yelling or confrontation actually pushes them further into that fight-or-flight nervous system response, creating further dysregulation.

This means the first step is to connect, heart to heart. A soft voice, listening, loving touch, and deep breathing are your biggest allies. If it feels right, give them a hug. If not, just be there for them as a strong, still presence. Get down to their level. As positive discipline expert Jane Nelsen says, it's vital to offer "connection before correction." When they have a tantrum, you get to be there and keep them safe. You're not fueling the tantrum and you aren't ignoring their suffering in that moment.

The connection goes back to safety, security, and warmth. Our children need to know and trust that we are there for them, no matter what. Connecting with them, just as they are, when things are rough lets them know that we are their home where they are always safe and welcome.

Checking and regulating our own nervous systems is therefore the vital first step. Our stable, regulated presence isn't always enough to help them find balance again, but it's the most important support we can offer.

STEP THREE: What's Really Happening?

When our kids melt down, it's easy to get caught up in our own assumptions, reactions, and emotions about the situation. When seven-year-olds hit their younger brothers or tweens scream "I hate you," our reactions are often to get defensive or to punish. What we really need in those situations is to pause and consider what's really going on.

Often, the behavior isn't actually the heart of the matter but a symptom of something else; it's the visible manifestation of something underneath the surface. Yes, we need to address the behavior, but first we need to remember that all behaviors happen for a reason, perhaps a stress response, a feeling of isolation, growing pains, or discomfort. Whatever the specific reason, the behavior is a way for your child to get his needs met, one way or another.

It's helpful to see not just what is happening, but why. Asking ourselves what's motivating this action helps us see that they might be acting out for all sorts of reasons they can't verbalize. Children usually aren't screaming at us or fighting with siblings for the hell of it or to make us angry (even if it might feel that way sometimes). Things like hitting the baby or slamming the door don't come out of nowhere most of the time. They are almost always fueled by an intense emotion and/or a desire for connection. It might be fear, loneliness, or jealousy. How differently would we respond to our children hitting their baby siblings if we knew they just wanted us to say, "I love you and miss spending alone time together"?

We are trying to see arguing, slamming doors, eye rolling, yelling, hitting, or not doing homework as information rather than a problem. Instead of "What's wrong with you?" or *Why am I a terrible parent*, we can ask *What can I learn here? What's causing this behavior? What else is going on that's impacting this moment?* Instead of seeing unpleasant behaviors as attention seeking, it's often better to reframe them as connection seeking.

Once we start exploring what's really happening, we can connect to our long-term goals. Parenting experts Dan Siegel and Tina Bryson summarize this succinctly with three questions:

Why is this happening?

What lesson do I want to teach?

How am I going to teach it?

It's also helpful to ask questions of ourselves. *Am I taking this personally? Would I react the same way if I wasn't overwhelmed with work?* This allows us to see what's really going on, with them and us.

Once we reframe the behavior as a symptom—seeing it as an involuntary stress response rather than a deliberate sabotage or personal attack—it becomes much easier to respond with compassion. We remember that they are doing the best they can. Then we can decide how to help our children move toward greater well-being.

STEP FOUR: Help Them Self-Regulate

Here's a delightful paradox: You know those times when your kids are driving you the craziest? Those times that make you crazy in turn because you have no idea what to do and no clue what's going on? Those are actually the times when they need you most. When they are in meltdown mode, it's so easy to join them or feel triggered, but the truth is that they really need your help to soothe and self-regulate.

Self-regulation is about seeing and managing emotions and thoughts in a way that promotes a healthy response. It means identifying the causes of our outbursts and helping ourselves reduce the intensity or overreaction to certain stimuli. Everything we're already doing (empathizing, connecting, naming emotions) is all part of helping them regulate.

Focusing on self-regulation supports children to respond consciously rather than react automatically. We aren't trying to make everything happy, forcing calm, or ignoring the problem. We are providing a safe space in the moment so they can feel secure enough to be vulnerable and do what they need to find equilibrium.

In a heated moment, the best way to help them self-regulate is to speak softly and slowly and take deep breaths. Modeling deep breathing for them means they will likely—unconsciously—mirror you. Then, when things are calmer, focus on exploring self-regulation practices so they have those tools when they need them (see page 45).

STEP FIVE: Take Their Perspective

When your daughter comes home sobbing because a group of friends went to the mall without her, your automatic response might be, "You were just saying you don't like them. Maybe this is a good thing. Why would you want to go? You're better off." We say things like this with good intentions but it's also ignoring what they really need at that moment. They need us to see the situation from their perspective, affirm their feelings, and believe them.

We don't have to agree or even like what they say, but if we don't listen first, we've cost ourselves an opportunity for connection and we might inadvertently give the message that they should go to someone else when troubles arise.

Taking their perspective has two main, interconnected parts: listening and letting go of the script. Both involve empathy, open-mindedness, and compassion.

We want to listen as openly and nonjudgmentally as possible. When your son says that his teacher is mean or the class is too hard, he needs you to hear and believe him first despite your immediate interpretations. Then you can decide together how to proceed.

The second part asks us to let go of our expectations and affirm this moment as it is. This approach borrows from improv acting where the number one rule is to say "yes, and . . ." When one actor starts a scene with "Why are you wearing a tuxedo?" the other accepts the scene their partner is creating and adds to it: "It is my final night on your planet and I wanted to celebrate." Even when parents are trying to be affirming, we still often say "yes, but . . ." which cuts off connection and sometimes the conversation itself. "Yes, and" means *I hear and acknowledge what you're saying, and I'm going to build on it.*

When your nine-year-old demands a phone because all his friends have one, a "yes, but" response might sound like this: "That's fine for them, but they're not my child. You're too young." The "yes, and" response would be, "I hear you, and I imagine it's hard when everyone has a phone but you don't. Let's talk about it."

You can completely disagree with what your child is saying and still use "yes, and." The parent in the second option didn't buy the phone, but they connected and talked about it so the son felt understood, even if they didn't agree.

As you let go of the script, it's useful, once again, to check your expectations. What are your automatic reactions and assumptions? How can you notice those and still listen openly and affirm your child's needs at that moment?

STEP SIX: Acknowledge What's Happening and Validate Feelings

When your eight-year-old says she hates soccer and never wants to do it again, you might feel frustrated and annoyed. After all, it took forever to find the right team, fill out all the forms, and schlep her there with her little brother in tow. But when she's feeling upset or angry, what she really needs is for her feelings to be acknowledged and validated.

The main thing to remember is that all emotions are valid. We might not agree or understand them, but the truth of the moment is that our children are feeling something that needs care. Saying "There's nothing to be afraid of" might be true, but it's actually invalidating. It dismisses their real emotions, which can undermine their trust both in us and their own sense of what's happening. Instead, we want to be open to what they feel and let them know we believe them. "I hear you; you're scared. Being scared is scary, isn't it? Do you want to tell me about it?"

It's tempting to try to reason your child (or yourself) out of an emotion. This rarely works because emotions simply aren't logical. Think about it: Has anyone ever responded well to someone saying, "Oh, you shouldn't feel bad" or, "Don't worry. There's nothing to feel sad about"?

This step is all about letting go of reasons and focusing on feelings and connection. Even if your reaction is *But she loves soccer*, empathy should take precedence over logic in that moment.

Naming emotions comes in handy once again here. Giving emotions a name gives us the space to pause, see what's really happening, and decide what to do about it. As Siegel and Bryson say, we "name it to tame it." We acknowledge the feelings before trying to do anything about them.

As before, try to incorporate a "yes, and" approach. "I see that you're really upset, but you picked soccer" isn't actually validating the emotion. Try: "I see that you're really upset. And I want to work through this with you. How can we figure this out?"

Avoid "I know how you feel" statements. It's so much more welcoming to say, "I hear you saying that you don't like the coach." The latter encourages more conversation; the former limits it and can feel patronizing.

One final note here: all feelings are valid. All actions? Not so much. When your son hits his baby sister out of frustration, you can validate the feelings without validating the actions: "I can tell you're really angry right now. Being angry is okay, but hitting is not okay. What else could you do when you get angry?" There are no bad children and no bad feelings. Just more and less acceptable actions.

STEP SEVEN: Problem Solve Together

When we are stuck in an ongoing battle about healthy food, we need to quell our automatic tendency to lecture, yell, or blame (short-term obstacles) and focus on our long-term goals. Even the most challenging moments present opportunities to use problem solving and discipline to connect and guide our children toward well-being and flourishing.

Of course, the nature of the problem solving will depend on the situation, but the process is largely the same. Perhaps the most important step is to wait until everyone is ready. Then, focus on openly listening rather than lecturing, using as few words as possible while explaining your concern, and letting them take the lead as you work together to find a way forward.

Yes, it often feels easier if we come up with our own solutions or tell them the answer, but they don't usually listen when we lecture, and they grow and mature by wrestling with challenges and figuring things out for themselves. Once they do, they are more invested in the solution, so if something goes amiss, they learn responsibility and adaptability. Our job isn't to enforce or fix but to guide in an age-appropriate way.

Listening and letting them take the lead doesn't mean they make all the rules. Instead, it means that we get to demonstrate that we trust them (helping them to be trustworthy) and we're giving them the opportunity to be responsible, creative, problem-solving individuals.

When your kids refuse to eat what you prepared for dinner, your immediate reaction might be to tell them what to do or set an ultimatum. Instead, you want to sit down together and ask them what should happen next. Even if they don't know how to manage a situation, working on it together is imperative.

What does this look like?

First, with older kids, you can empower them by asking them for the best time to speak about the issue, suggesting two or three times that work. When you do sit down to talk, you might start by saying you've noticed the situation—name it—and want to hear their thoughts on it. State the problem as simply and nonjudgmentally as possible: "I notice that we argue a lot about food." Then pause and let them talk. Listen to their version of things and acknowledge how they feel. You can share your reasoning and perspective as well, recognizing they might not agree. Then ask, "How would you like to handle this?" or "How can we handle this together?" making sure listening comes before responding.

Together, you can brainstorm, writing down every idea, even the craziest ones. Once you have a list, you can work together to figure out which ones fit for both of you, using the skills from previous chapters in this discussion. After listening openly, explain your view with clear reasons. If their solution is "I never eat vegetables again," you can respond with, "I'm hearing that you don't like eating vegetables. It's important to eat a healthy diet because that gives you nutrients to grow your brain and do things you love, like gymnastics. What other ideas could we try?"

Problem solving is where we finally get to address the challenging behavior. In doing so, it's not us versus them. We are a team working together with the aim of helping our children flourish and problem solve for themselves.

STEP EIGHT: Use Consequences That Fit

Once you've gone through all these steps, come back to the rules and expectations of the household. Consequences are still important. Positive discipline allows us to use consequences as a teaching tool rather than as punishment or to make children pay.

The tools and consequences should fit with your overall goals and should connect directly to the situation. You are helping teach them that their actions matter and that you trust them to take responsibility. When your child throws food, the consequence might be cleaning up the food before being able to play after dinner. If nothing happens, or if you clean it up, they learn they can get away with it. If too much happens (the punishment doesn't fit the so-called crime), they might become resentful or mistrustful.

You might have come up with a solution already while problem solving in step 7. If not, consider asking them here, too, though you are the final arbiter: "What do you think should happen next? How could you make things right with your sister? How can you help pay for the new hockey stick?" Then, whatever you decide together, make sure you follow through consistently.

Focus on listening rather than talking. It's tempting to lecture, but as anyone who has ever been lectured to knows, it's just not effective. Instead, let them take the lead and responsibility for solving the issue.

More Supports for Positive Discipline in Your Home

Here are some more specific strategies that promote good habits and foster stronger connections so you can avoid some of the more serious meltdowns.

Give notifications: You know your five-year-old never wants to leave the playground. So, help him as much as you can by telling him what's going on. Give him warnings: five minutes left, one minute left, etc. Or offer options: "You can have two more minutes or one more game."

Don't ask questions that lead to negative answers: In trying to avoid the battle of wills, it's helpful to give them opportunities to succeed. When you know your ten-year-old hasn't made her bed, don't ask, "Have you made your bed?" This can lead to lying, frustration, and/or disappointment. Instead, give her the chance to succeed: "What else do you need to do to get ready this morning?"

Food, exercise, sleep: These issues are obviously bigger than the scope of positive parenting, but they remain important to keep in mind. Anyone else get hangry? We feel like the whole world is against us, but it turns out we just needed food. Our kids are the same way. They might be getting emotional or upset not because of what's actually happening but because they are tired, hungry, or haven't had enough time outside or exercise. If your child keeps losing it at the grocery store, one common culprit is being overtired or hungry.

Be creative: Creativity works wonders, especially with younger children. In our house, instead of "Eat your breakfast" we say, "Eat the food that's the squarest" or "Find the food that looks most like Daddy." When you need your children to leave the store, instead of the usual, "Time to go," you might try "Let's see who can take the fewest steps to get to the door."

Give choices and/or let them make decisions: Give them options, both of which are acceptable to you. Saying "Don't run in the house" doesn't give them a sense of what they *should* do. Instead try: "You can run outside or you can draw inside." Letting them make decisions can be as simple as asking your toddler if he wants the blue or the red shirt. Doing so helps him practice decision making, thus training his brain for it. Giving choices also demonstrates that you respect and trust your children and eliminates fights that come from demands. When we say, "Drink your milk," "No" comes out almost naturally. But "Are you going to have five sips or forty-seven?" combines a fun approach with a chance for them to feel like they're in charge.

With older kids, be genuine with the choices you offer and give them opportunities to exercise their free will and take responsibility. Instead of nagging about chores, ask them how they are going to make sure everything gets done. Let older children set their own schedules (within reason, of course). Nagging them to do homework just makes everyone feel bad. Encouraging them to be in charge of their own time can make a world of difference and fosters trust and responsibility.

Enlist their help: Most children love to be in charge or to know that you trust them to be responsible, one way or another. When you're trying to get everyone out the door, tell them you need their help. Be specific. "Would you carry my bag?" or "Please grab your jacket from the closet."

Be kind *and* firm: We aren't letting them walk all over us and we aren't taskmasters. They need to know that we're open to what they're going through and what they say, but also that we aren't pushovers.

Take breaks: Your children need breaks and so do you. When everything is coming to a head or everyone's getting frustrated, go for a walk, take a breather, or have a one-minute dance party. Come back or reconvene when everyone feels okay doing so.

BUILD MINDFULNESS AND
SELF-REGULATION TOOLS

As noted, it's helpful to practice using self-regulation tools when things are relatively calm so children have those tools when they really need them. Here are some more tactics you can try:

- Build time into your daily schedule to stop and take a few deep breaths together. Make it a routine: one breath before leaving for school and one before bedtime. For little children, you can encourage this with songs focused on taking a breath (see page 145). You can also adapt any of the practices from chapter 3.

- Encourage them to notice and name their emotions throughout the day. You can download age-appropriate lists or charts to help them build a vocabulary, making emotions easier to identify. Help them by asking them to rate their feelings on a scale from 1 to 10 or by using emojis to represent what they feel. For little children, encourage them to draw their feelings, represent them as a color or animal, or act them out.

- Help them create a plan for the next time they get upset. "I noticed you want to hit when you're upset. Can we come up with something safer for you to hit, like a pillow?"

- Normalize stopping and taking breaks when needed. Model this for them. Say aloud, "I'm feeling really frustrated; I'm just going to stop and give myself a break."

- Encourage them to move their bodies and go outside as needed.

- Build a peace zone, regulation station, or a calm-down kit. Find things you could put into a special box or corner that anyone in the family can use when they start to feel overwhelmed. You could incorporate flowers, notes, stuffed animals, poems, or quotes.

- Try muscle relaxation. The basic idea is to tense up your muscles and then let go, relaxing as much as possible. You can do this with your entire body at once or start at your toes and work your way up each body part.

- Make a glitter jar. There are lots of links for this on the web. A child shakes the jar so the glitter is whirling everywhere. Then they sit and watch the glitter settle, breathing and imagining that their feelings or thoughts are settling, too.

- Explore the 5-4-3-2-1 Grounding Exercise. Have your children look for five things they can see, four things they can feel, three things they can hear, two things they can smell, and one thing they can taste. This exercise is particularly good for anxiety.

Strengths-Based Parenting

Positive parenting is not meant to be a one-size-fits-all solution. In fact, it's not meant to be a "solution" at all, per se. The idea is to approach things in a different way, one where our unhelpful habits get less focus and greater attention is placed on what helps us shine.

Some of the obstacles to our success are the natural tendencies of our brains. Our brains are hardwired to see the negative more than the positive, a phenomenon called the negativity bias. And not just to see the negative but also to notice it, remember it, and give more weight to it. It's evolutionarily wired into us all. It made sense when we needed to scan our environment for threats constantly. It causes problems, however, because it's so easy to lose sight of everything but the negative, so we need to work extra hard to make the positive stand out. John Gottman, a well-known researcher and marriage therapist, found that we actually need five positive things for every one negative thing in order to help the positive stick out more.

The more we practice seeing the good—strengths, love, sweet moments, and connections—the better our brains get at seeing them, identifying them, remembering them, and overcoming negativity bias. Strengths-based parenting takes this even further. Martin Seligman and his associates found that focusing on human strengths acts as a buffer against mental illness. In fact, identifying and emphasizing strengths can help enhance overall well-being and improve relationships.

Through their extensive research, Dr. Seligman and Dr. Peterson found six virtues and 24 strengths that not only exist to some degree in every individual but also exist across almost every culture in the world. Their book *Character Strengths and Virtues* describes the list as follows (with the virtues listed first and their associated strengths following):

Wisdom and knowledge: creativity, curiosity, judgment, love of learning, perspective

Courage: bravery, honesty, persistence, zest

Humanity: love, kindness, social intelligence

Justice: fairness, leadership, teamwork

Temperance: forgiveness, humility, prudence, self-regulation

Transcendence: appreciation of beauty and excellence, gratitude, hope, humor, spirituality

As you look at this list, take some time to consider what your children's strengths are. What are they good at? What strengths could they nurture and grow? These aren't their talents, skills, or interests but rather qualities and moral traits that can be cultivated and learned and that require effort. These likely relate back to your long-term goals and will definitely help your children pursue those goals.

As we consider our children's strengths, perspective becomes particularly important.

My daughter seems to have selective hearing. If she's reading a book and I call her for dinner or even sit down next to her, she just doesn't hear or notice me. Does it drive me crazy? Yes. But does that also mean she has an unbelievable ability to focus, that she loves learning, and that she's persistent? Again, yes. Maybe your youngest is always frustrated that his brother gets more than he does or that everything isn't equal. Or he's always late because he wants to do everything meticulously? Yes, we can see those as negatives. But we will help ourselves and our children so much more if we can find the related strengths, such as fairness, teamwork, or appreciation of beauty and excellence.

If it's helpful, you might fill out the chart below. Write down a particular action or behavior. Consider how you might interpret it automatically (often negatively). Now, how can it be reframed as a strength?

BEHAVIOR	AUTOMATIC INTERPRETATION	REFRAMED AS STRENGTH

BEHAVIOR	AUTOMATIC INTERPRETATION	REFRAMED AS STRENGTH

Once you start to pay attention to strengths, you can use this knowledge to bolster all the work you are doing with positive parenting. Lea Waters, a leading voice in this field, shares some suggestions for how to implement these ideas in your home.

Strengths spotting: Like the activity above, this involves identifying and emphasizing your child's strengths. Share them aloud as much as possible: "You showed such good judgment and forward thinking today when you decided to save your money for what you really wanted." "Your room is decorated so beautifully. I love your creativity and new ideas. What will you try next?" As Waters points out, this is especially helpful because of our neuroplastic brain. The more you offer these acknowledgments, the more the child will internalize them. (This is a very helpful practice to do for yourself and your partner, too.)

As you spot these strengths, make sure to emphasize how your children are working at them: trying new things, learning, and strengthening their brains all the time. Praising strengths avoids the pitfalls of a fixed mindset because the focus is on effort, learning, and engagement.

Daily strengths check-in: Instead of "How was school?" try asking, "What strengths did you use today?" For younger children, you might prompt a bit more: "How did you help someone today? What did you work really hard at today? What made you smile today?" If something went amiss, ask, "Which strengths could you use next time?"

Strengths map: Map out the strengths of the whole family. (This can be a family activity where each member lists strengths of the others.) Then create opportunities to use these strengths in and out of the home. "We have guests coming over for dinner. Would you like to use your creativity to make place cards?"

Strengths-based questions: If your children are worried about an upcoming test or any challenge, ask them how they can use their strengths to study or feel more confident.

When you start to pay more attention to their strengths, it becomes easier to see all the ways that things are going right rather than all the ways they aren't. It allows us to appreciate our children and the moments we have with them for who and what they are.

Conclusion

Books can provide tools and ideas, but to make positive parenting really fit your home and family, you have to find your own approach. Some of what's here will resonate; some of it won't. A lot of it will seem weird or impossible until you give it a try and figure out how it works for you and your children. When I started, I firmly thought there was no way that my kid would respond well to these suggestions. But once we found our own language and approach, it really has made a difference.

SELF-CARE BREAK: Self-Compassion

We can say it again and again: Being a parent is not easy. There will be times when you feel like you're failing. And it doesn't matter how many times someone (or some book) tells you that it's okay to make mistakes, it still sucks. So it can be really helpful to try some self-compassion.

Most of us are experts at self-criticism. It's deeply ingrained and one of the hardest habits to change. Dr. Kristin Neff teaches that self-compassion has three main components: kindness, mindfulness, and common humanity. We connect to these qualities to give ourselves some much needed care.

1. Start by taking a few deep breaths. Notice what it feels like to be you right now. Do your best to let the feeling be without judging it or trying to get rid of it even if what you're feeling is really hard.
2. You might need to remind yourself that it's okay to take this time for yourself.
3. If you have time, begin with a short breath meditation or take a moment to release any obvious tension in your body. This can help settle your mind a bit, giving you a chance to be with the self-compassion practice.
4. Imagine you could breathe in kindness and compassion and breathe out anything that's not helping you right now.
5. In your mind, say some of the following phrases (or ones you create for yourself).

   » Kindness: "I'm okay." "I don't have to solve this right now." "I wish to be peaceful." "I love myself."

» Mindfulness: "I'm really suffering right now." "This moment is really hard." "This hurts."

» Common humanity: "I'm not alone." "There is nothing wrong with me." "Other people feel this way, too."

6. It can be helpful to imagine someone you love or someone who loves you giving you a hug and saying the phrases with or to you.

7. As much as possible, let go of the need to fix or solve whatever arises as you do this exercise. Instead, just try to let yourself be cared for by those phrases and intentions. If it brings up tears or judgments, that's okay. Imagine holding yourself the way you hold your children when they are in pain, giving yourself the care you would give them.

8. Take a few more deep breaths and let yourself feel supported.

If this feels phony or fake, don't worry. It's a natural response, and you aren't doing it wrong. If you can do it anyway, you'll probably find it makes a difference, regardless of how it feels at first.

Self-compassion isn't about getting rid of painful feelings. The intention is to be kind and gentle to ourselves *just as we are while things are hard*. You might find your own phrases that resonate for you. You can even use phrases you regularly share with your children, like "I love you to the moon and back."

CHAPTER 6

Positive Parenting in Action

FAQ FOR WHEN THINGS GO SIDEWAYS

You've probably noticed that we refer to things going "sideways" when describing those moments when everything feels off, out of control, or unexpected. This deliberate word choice is an important part of positive parenting because the approach asks us to reframe behavior as more or less pleasant or challenging rather than as right or wrong or good or bad. When we interpret a situation or action as wrong, we can close ourselves off to what our children really need from us at that time. It's not wrong when they act up. In a sense it's actually right because that's what their brains, cognitive development, and nervous systems are bound to do at their age and stage. These sideways moments aren't bad; they are just less pleasant or more challenging, often because we don't expect them.

In this chapter, we'll share several FAQ and scenarios to which most parents can relate, and we'll discuss possible ways to approach these scenarios.

Q. *All this positive discipline stuff sounds great, but sometimes I just need my children to listen. I hate nagging and yelling, but sometimes it feels like I have to. How do I stop the arguing and get them to listen to what I say?*

A. One thing you might reflect on with this question is: Are you asking them to listen or are you asking them to obey? A lot of the time when we talk about listening or cooperation, we are actually hoping for obedience or conformity. Once we start to recognize this, we can let go of the focus on obedience and instead concentrate our efforts on harmony, cooperation, and respect.

Most of us know that yelling into the other room rarely yields the response we want. We yell "Come for dinner." They yell "Just a minute." The minute passes and we yell again. This easily escalates to arguing and mutual frustration. If we're just barking orders and expecting to be obeyed, we're not really modeling good communication. If we want them to listen, we need to walk the walk. Oftentimes, children will listen when they are listened to.

When you need them to hear you, focus on connecting first. Start with a knock on their bedroom door or a simple inquiry like "What show are you watching?" You want to try to see things from their perspective. Yes, you want the table set but they're busy playing. No one likes to stop playing and do chores, kids or adults. Help them by offering choices. "Do you need two more minutes or three? Would you like me to set a timer or do you want to do it?"

Focus on lecturing less and on empathizing more. Parents usually talk and lecture too much, and children simply tune us out (just like we did to our parents and teachers). Instead of lecturing, ask short, simple questions that give them an opportunity to solve problems and think creatively: "How could you help solve this problem? What do you think?" Parenting experts Farber and Mazlich also recommend using very short descriptions: "I see dirty clothes on the floor."

When you do speak, you want to offer specific reasons why something needs to be done. You are helping them understand the rationale behind the action, which might include their safety, health, well-being, caring for themselves or others, specific time restraints, or external rules. So, it's not just "Don't swing the bat!" but "That looks like fun. It can also really hurt someone. What else could you play with?"

Children need and want their own autonomy. Their recalcitrance is often a sign that they're testing out their independence, an important milestone that we want them to achieve. Consider how you can enlist their cooperation. When you need to leave the house and your youngest starts grabbing her finger paints, take a moment to see things from her perspective: "I want to finger paint, too! Let's think of a time we could do that together."

We also want to go back to that perennial parenting advice to pick our battles. We want to use demands sparingly so they have impact when we need them to.

Nagging usually comes when we are trying to control too much or trying to control what we can't control. I found this out the hard way with the morning routine in our house. I was trying to be on top of everything and it was making everyone, especially me, crazy. Instead of "Eat your breakfast, have you eaten your breakfast, drink your milk, etc., etc.," now we go with "You are in charge of getting yourself ready. What do you need to do? How are you going to make sure you get out the door in time?" When we approach it this way, not only do our children get to practice responsibility, but nagging is no longer the default way anything gets accomplished. (Note, this doesn't happen magically. Our mornings may be full of reminders and helpful cues, but the onus is on the child not the parent.)

Other phrases you might try:

- What do you need to do?

- Would you like to do it yourself or would you like help?

- What's the best way you could do this?

- Make your bed like a bunny/artist/the color blue.

- We're on sprinter time or cheetah time.

Q. *Okay, but what about a teen or tween in full-on rebellion mode? My formerly gentle, loving 13-year-old has turned into someone I barely recognize. She's not doing her homework, doesn't want to be with the rest of the family, and spends all her time hunched over her phone. She came home a few days ago with purple hair and I know her peer group is experimenting with all sorts of things I wasn't expecting for at least a few more years. Help!*

A. A lot of the time when kids start rebelling or making more of their own choices, our impulse as parents is to try to rein things in. We feel out of control, so we try to gain more control. It usually works against us, not for us. What you're probably finding is that the more you nag, threaten, and/or punish, the more friction, struggle, and disagreement there is, right?

It's really hard for us, but what she's doing is an important part of growing up. She's finding her individuality and own perspective, part of which means distancing herself from you. Even though we all know this will happen, we often aren't prepared for how jarring it can be when it happens to us.

That doesn't mean you do nothing. You want to focus on unconditional love, empathy, and keeping things in perspective while believing in her and connecting in whatever way fits best.

First, keep assuring her that you love her no matter what. It doesn't matter if she appears to be listening or not. It doesn't matter if she says it back. She will hear you and know you are there for her when she needs you. (It also doesn't matter if she's driving you crazy at the time. That's what teenagers do. We still want to love them unconditionally.)

Do your best to see things from her perspective. She has a million things going on in her brain and few of those are helping her feel grounded or make good decisions. Empathy matters here. When you're having the homework battle for the hundredth time, stop for a moment and consider: You care about grades, but does she? What is it like to have friends who are bullying or telling her that studying is lame? This doesn't mean that she gets to stop studying because she doesn't care, just that you are bridging the gap between your perspective and hers.

Remember that this is an obstacle. It won't last forever. And it's not about you. Parents tend to take it personally that the relationship has changed or worry there is something wrong with their children. This is a phase. Just like teething, potty training, and that period when my daughter managed to hit me in the nose every single day, this too shall pass.

When struggles do come up, try to avoid doing or solving anything when either of you is agitated. Wait. Take a breather and come back later. It's okay to go to bed mad if you both need the space. Then try to give her some control or agency. Ask her when would be a good time to talk about it and provide a few options of times that might work.

When you do meet, let her take the lead. Instead of starting with a long diatribe, it's much more empowering to give her space to share her perspective first. From my experience teaching teenagers and young adults, I can tell you that the more I talk, the less they do. (Also, the more I talk, the less they listen.)

Teens need warmth and structure, too. They need you in their lives but not controlling their lives. They need to know they can count on you. How do you do this? Take a genuine interest in what she is doing, not so you can hang out with her all the time but so you are connected, showing her that you understand and care. Spend time together in whatever way feels comfortable for the two of you, even if it's just in the car on the way to pick up a younger sibling. Ask her why she chose purple for her hair, maybe even ask if she would color yours, too. Let your daughter invite her friends over. This isn't so you can supervise but so she has a reliable and secure place to hang out. You're connecting with her as she is and showing her that you trust her. She won't stop being rebellious, but she knows she has a safe place to do so.

Q. *Shopping is a nightmare. My daughter (age four) loves to pull everything off the grocery store shelves while my son (age eight) spends the entire time asking for things. I have tried saying no and reasoning with them, but I feel like I've lost control of the situation.*

A. Sometimes it feels like shopping brings out the worst in all of us. Fortunately, there are things you can do with each of your children. Seeing things from their perspectives, getting them involved, and validating feelings should all offer some help.

For a moment, put yourself in their shoes. Your daughter is likely excited and overwhelmed by everything she sees. She's not trying to upset you; she just wants to play, and it's very hard for her to remember in the moment that she shouldn't touch. After all, touching and exploring everything is what preschoolers do best. Meanwhile, your son is somewhat at the mercy of companies that pay millions precisely to get him to want their stuff.

First, make sure you aren't shopping when they are hungry. A snack in the car can be helpful if you need to shop right after school or before dinner. Next, your daughter needs something to do. There's just too much temptation otherwise. Get her involved. Give her the shopping list and a crayon and have her check off items one by one. Ask her to be your important helper, pointing to the reddest apple or the squarest box of crackers. You can help her feel important and empowered and get her using and training her brain.

Reasoning with her isn't going to work because her brain is just not that logical, and in the moment, she's too distracted to pay attention. Keep explanations very short. "Apples don't like being touched" or "Fingers spread germs."

You might do a trial run at home, practicing being in "aisles" with her. Since most children love to be in charge and role-play, ask her to show her favorite stuffed animal how to behave in the supermarket.

With your son, try acknowledging and understanding his perspective (without changing your boundaries). Although it makes perfect sense to you, explaining why he can't have something doesn't actually address his feelings. Next time he wants something, you might try asking him to tell you about it: "Why do you want that toy or that candy? What made you choose that one?" You can also affirm his feelings: "Yeah, that looks awesome. I can see why you'd want that. Imagine if we had a whole room full!" Then, do something that lets him know that you hear him. "Why don't we write it down so we can remember when it's time for your birthday?" or "Let's take a picture so we can keep it in mind when you have enough money from your allowance." For candy, you might put him in charge: "You're allowed to pick out one treat for the next two weeks. Is this the one you want?"

Depending on his age and maturity, you might use this to start a discussion about the power of marketing, helping him cultivate awareness of the many unsolicited messages he takes in each day. Without getting too serious, you can explain that characters on food boxes are designed to make him feel a particular way so he will want to buy that product. You could ask: "Why is there a bunny on that box? What do bunnies have to do with cereal?" Discussions like these encourage critical thinking and smarter choices. The next time he sees an ad on TV or the internet, you can explain that advertisers' jobs are to make us feel insecure so we will buy their products. It's a great lead-in to exploring and encouraging self-confidence, how he is good enough just as he is.

If struggles continue, have a discussion when you're away from the store. Explain that you are feeling frustrated and ask them for ideas on how you can all make grocery shopping easier.

Q. *What do I do about lying? I catch my children in little and not-so-little lies all the time and it drives me crazy.*

A. Catching children lying can be very frustrating, especially when you prize honesty and communication in your home. And yet, as with the other challenges, it's helpful to put lying into perspective. Early childhood lying is actually a developmental milestone. It shows that your youngster has "theory of mind," which is the ability to recognize that her own mind sees and experiences different things than other people's. When your four-year-old tells a fib, she's demonstrating her developing consciousness and greater understanding of the world.

Older kids lie for all sorts of reasons, many of which are understandable when broken down. They might avoid telling you the truth because they are ashamed, don't want to get in trouble, or don't want to disappoint you. Often, they lie because they are scared of letting you down. Seeing it from that point of view, their motivation is totally understandable even if the behavior drives you crazy.

So, what can you do? First, you want to be kind and firm, balancing structure and warmth. This means avoiding yelling or blaming while empathizing and sticking to the rules of the house. You want to focus on connection while using questions to help them tell the truth or admit the falsehoods. Instead of "Did you make your bed?" you might say, "I see that you haven't made your bed yet. What's your plan for that this morning?" Instead of "Did you use my makeup?" when you know they did, you might say, "I see that my makeup is out. Let's talk about what the rules are again."

Being as forthright as possible will help as well. Don't say, "You can tell me anything and I promise you won't get in trouble" when you know that will be an impossible promise to keep. Instead you might emphasize how consequences will follow because those are the rules of the house *and* the consequences will be much worse if they lie. You can be honest yourself when you say, "I can't promise I won't get angry. I can promise that I will get a lot less angry if you tell me the truth."

It's also supportive to praise honesty whenever it's present, even making it a much bigger deal than you might otherwise. Every time there is honest communication, make a note of it. "Thank you for being so honest with me."

If the lying continues with older children or adolescents, you might need to address it directly. Again, try to see things from their perspective while avoiding lecturing. Share that you are concerned and that you hope they know they can tell you anything.

Q. *I feel guilty asking this, but I need help with the fact that my child wants to be with me all the time. He's only five and I know I should appreciate these moments while I have them. But he's always climbing on top of me when I'm trying to work or asking a million questions when I'm on the phone. I don't mean to get frustrated, but I do. How do I set boundaries without hurting his feelings?*

A. Isn't it great how even the most wonderful aspects of having children can still become an issue? One thing you're already doing well is recognizing that his intentions are good and that he loves you, even if his clambering all over you at all times might get frustrating. You're also recognizing your own automatic reaction and doing your best to explore a different response.

Here, it's helpful to set some clear boundaries for him and for yourself: together time and alone time. You can explain that it's important to you to give all your attention to one thing (thereby modeling focus and presence). When you're with him, you don't want to have to pay attention to work; you just want to be with him. And sometimes, when you have to work or when you're socializing, you want to give all your attention to that. When he is clamoring for attention, you can tell him, "I want to give you all my attention and I have to do this first. How about we play together in 10 minutes?" Then make sure you give him specific choices for what he could do next so that he has a designated activity while you are occupied.

It's also helpful to give him attention soon after you get home from work or after you have been apart for the day. Even if it's just 10 minutes to play or connect, do your best to give him your full attention. Then, you can honestly tell him, "Sweetie, I need to go answer some emails right now. I am going to give that my full attention so I can finish quickly, and then we can have dinner together."

Likewise, make sure you are focused on him when you are playing together. When work crops up or you have the urge to check your emails, set those boundaries for yourself. It isn't easy, especially when you have demands from your boss, but you are demonstrating valuable skills and strengths for him to emulate and allowing yourself to fully appreciate your time together.

One other thing you can try is "working" together: "I need to get this done. How about we read alongside each other?" This might not go as well at age five as age 10, but you're setting the stage for a future of connection.

Even when work or social obligations get overwhelming, try to make sure you are setting aside special time just for the two of you. If you are truly swamped, you could mark it on a calendar with a big colorful circle or set out paper and markers and start to dream up and draw out ideas for your big afternoon next Sunday.

Q. *How do I get my son to apply himself? He's smart and capable but he just loafs on the couch all the time. I know he gets invited out with friends, but he doesn't go. His siblings are active and hanging out with friends. How can I help him?*

A. We all want the best for our children. Sometimes, however, we are imposing our version of what's best onto them rather than letting them dictate what it means for them. Each child is unique, wanting and needing to be seen and accepted for who they are. Your other children might be extroverts, thriving on social connection. Your son might be an introvert, needing more quiet and more time by himself to recharge. Since you don't mention that your son seems unhappy or troubled, it's possible that this is just who he is. He might just really like being alone and quiet. What he needs is for you to see things from his perspective and support him.

When I worked with adolescent figure skaters, one of their most commonly expressed wishes was that their parents would just listen to them. They would say, "My mom pushes me so hard" or "My dad cares more about the competition than I do." These young athletes just wanted someone to love them no matter what and really be there for them as they are. Your son will thrive with that approach, too. He might appreciate you just sitting on the couch next to him, both of you reading, or going for a walk together. Admittedly, he might not want that at all. Let him take the lead.

Q. *I'm worried about my daughter. She has always been very sensitive. It seems like she takes everything to heart and gets derailed by even the slightest mistake. I try to tell her that it's okay or that she did her best, but she's just so hard on herself and gets terribly upset so easily. How do I deal with such a sensitive child?*

A. As someone who used to be that highly sensitive child, too perfectionistic and emotional for my own good, this question really hits home. There are a few ways you can support your daughter to build resilience while also helping her recognize and even befriend her emotions.

First, you can emphasize how everyone makes mistakes. It's helpful to model your own mistakes. Be vocal about how something went sideways at work or how you had to apologize to someone else. This isn't about giving her specific lessons but rather about normalizing failure. You could name sports stars or artistic heroes who have been very forthcoming about their failures, people like J. K. Rowling, Jay-Z, Michael Jordan, and Oprah. Many inventions came as a result of "mistakes," including chocolate chip cookies and penicillin!

One way to help her build resilience is to focus on praising effort, and, in particular, learning. As parents, we often fall into common traps when we say things like "All you have to do is try" or "Not everyone can be good at everything." These can actually undermine learning and resilience. Instead we want to normalize that mistakes happen and what's important is to forgive ourselves and explore what we can learn from the mistakes or what we can do next. Failure is not a demonstration of who we are. It's an opportunity to see what we can do next.

You might encourage more focus on process rather than success. Ask her: "What are you most proud of? Which part did you work hardest at?" This can help her build her own internal motivation and self-efficacy.

The next piece is to encourage her to practice self-compassion and mindfulness, both of which will help increase her awareness of the patterns of her mind. Once she can see those habits with kindness and compassion, then she can see whether they are helpful or not. When she's in the thick of an emotion, her most terrible thoughts feel so real and true. Doing these practices will help her get some space from those thoughts and feelings so, over time, she can change how she identifies with them.

Validating feelings is especially important with sensitive children. Remind her that it's okay not to be okay, that she's not alone, and that being a kid and growing up can be really hard at times. It's helpful to create a vocabulary around emotions and feelings. With younger children, you can talk about moods and feelings like the weather: "Is it sunny or cloudy inside?" As they get older, you can explore or create a feelings wheel or chart that lists hundreds of different feelings. This will help them give a name to what's going on, which supports them in seeing that they aren't alone in feeling this way.

In my experience, most kids love learning about their brains. You might explore neuroplasticity with her, sharing the idea that she has the power to change the abilities and structure of her brain. Children appreciate learning that they can get better at qualities like patience and happiness just like they can get better at piano or karate. These lessons can have a truly radical impact as Carol Dweck discovered in her classroom when one particularly disruptive boy asked, "You mean I don't have to be dumb?"

Finally, help her find or create a peaceful place in the house. It can be a corner of her room, on the balcony, in the backyard, or just a special cushion she can sit on. Encourage her to decorate or arrange it so it feels safe, inviting, and soothing. It doesn't have to be fancy or expensive. It's just a quiet, safe place for her to go so she can help herself feel less overwhelmed by those powerful thoughts and feelings.

Q. *Positive parenting makes sense to me but others around me don't agree. My question is: How do I get my parents—the grandparents—on board? They're more of the "do as I say" type.*

A. In an ideal world, everyone who encounters your kids would be on the same page when it comes to positive discipline. In reality, you will probably have to be a bit more patient and do a lot more communicating in order to get some people on board.

I got a good lesson in this a while ago after I took an extra 10 minutes to comfort, connect, and brainstorm solutions with my daughter after she was upset about something that happened at school. To be honest, I had been quite proud of myself at that moment because I didn't get frustrated or feel rushed. I had been really listening to her, validating her feelings, and helping her figure out her own solutions to the issue.

But when I relayed the story to acquaintances, they scoffed at me, saying that my daughter was just pushing my buttons and taking advantage of me. Even though I knew I had done what I wanted and what my daughter needed at that time, I still felt hurt.

It's impossible to get everyone to agree on anything, let alone something as important as taking care of children. Your parents might say that you need to be firmer or that a child's job is to listen. The best thing you can do in those situations is remind yourself of your goals and the tools you've been practicing. Take a moment and a breath, giving yourself time to self-regulate and recognizing that your parents are trying their best and aren't purposefully angering you.

Then, as succinctly as possible, share (with those who will listen, because not everyone will) what this approach is all about and why you're doing it. You might let them know that you see discipline as a way to teach rather than punish, and that it's important to you that your child's feelings are always validated, even though his actions won't always be acceptable. You can share your long-term goals and explain that whenever anything goes sideways, you try to see the behavior as a symptom and that you ask yourself what's motivating the behavior and consider how discipline can help you reach those goals. You might explain that you're trying to create an environment where everyone in the family feels heard, respected, and safe. You might share the steps in chapter 5 or your intention to respond thoughtfully to what's really happening in the moment rather than reacting automatically.

You can assure your parents that you know they have your child's best interests at heart and, at the same time, that these are the rules of your household. As with our children, we want to be kind and firm. Your parents are more likely to hear you if you listen to and respect them. At the same time, this is your household, and your rules matter.

In my experience, one of the best ways to get anyone on board is to share some of the brain science with them. If you tell other people that you want your three-year-old to make decisions, you'll likely get some funny looks. But if you say you are letting your three-year-old make small, doable decisions because you want him to exercise his executive function, thereby building his prefrontal cortex so he can build his ability to self-regulate, not many people will argue with you. Often, people will be persuaded by science when your own reasoning doesn't satisfy them.

Conclusion

A friend of mine who worked as a ski instructor told me that the first thing novice skiers learn is how to fall. (Personally, I've never needed help falling, but she's the expert.) The reasoning is that you learn how to fall in a controlled environment so that you have the skills when you really need them. This is similar to how I teach meditation. The goal isn't to be great at meditating but to practice when things are relatively calm and still so that we have tools for when nothing feels calm or still. So much of positive parenting follows this model. The way we interact with our kids on a daily basis builds the skills to succeed when tantrums, arguments, and challenges come to a head. Positive parenting isn't a one-time solution or something we use instead of punishment. It's a way of being that promotes better relationships, more integrity, and more flourishing in the long run.

It's helpful to remember that this is a process. We talked about fostering a growth mindset in our children, and we need it, too. We need to remember that there are always opportunities to grow, learn, and change. Until some distant future when robots take over our brains, we will continue to make mistakes. Positive parenting isn't about getting parenting "right" or doing everything perfectly. It's about being open to and real with what's happening to our kids and ourselves. It's keeping the bigger picture in mind so the obstacles don't derail us as much, and approaching ourselves and our children with compassion and patience.

Positive parenting helps me love my child for who and how she is, while still encouraging and nurturing her growth and maturity. I love quiet. She's not all that familiar with the concept. Sure, it gets on my nerves at times. But wanting or expecting her to be *fundamentally* different just makes us both unhappy. Embracing her as she is helps set the conditions for us all to thrive.

Being a parent is hard enough without getting caught up in unrealistic expectations of how things should be or blaming ourselves when things don't go a particular way. The positive parenting approach offers us some freedom from those "shoulds," which is especially helpful because, as we all know, things almost never go the way we think they "should." As parents, it's actually not our job to *make* our children happy, which is good because we can't force emotions on them or anyone else. And it's not their job to make us happy, either. Positive parenting tools and strategies help us set the optimal conditions for everyone to find their own happiness and well-being, even if what that looks like and how we get there are a lot different than what we might have expected.

And for all the parents, guardians, grandparents, relatives, and caregivers out there: You're doing great.

Perhaps the best parenting advice I've received was to call everything a phase. From teething to sleep regressions, growth spurts to emotional upheaval, it was eminently helpful to be reminded that it would not last forever. Our minds naturally glom on to the challenge of the moment and invariably decide that it's going to be that way forever and we'll never endure. If we can be reminded that it will come to an end, then we know we can get through it, even if it's hard.

Whatever you are feeling, whatever stress you are experiencing, however challenging this moment is, or however your children are or are not being respectful, do your best to see it and call it a phase. It can be helpful to notice how everything is changing all the time: sounds, thoughts, sensations, feelings, and moods. Try to recall the last "this is never going to end" phase and remember that you got through that, too. Combining this practice with some self-compassion can be truly beneficial in those particularly rough phases, reminding you that they don't last forever.

RESOURCES

Below you'll find a list of books, websites, and songs or videos that will help you further develop your mindfulness and positive discipline skills.

Books

Ain't Misbehavin' by Alyson Schafer

Authentic Happiness: Using the New Positive Psychology to Realize Your Potential for Lasting Fulfillment by Martin Seligman

Building Resilience in Children and Teens: Giving Kids Roots and Wings by Kenneth Ginsburg

How to Talk So Kids Will Listen and Listen So Kids Will Talk by Adele Farber and Elaine Mazlish

If I Have to Tell You One More Time... by Amy McCready

Inventing Ourselves: The Secret Life of the Teenage Brain by Sarah-Jayne Blakemore

Kids These Days by Jody Carrington

Mindful Parenting in a Chaotic World by Nicole Libin

Mindset: The New Psychology of Success by Carol S. Dweck

No Drama Discipline: The Whole-Brain Way to Calm the Chaos and Nurture Your Child's Developing Mind and The Whole-Brain Child: 12 Revolutionary Strategies to Nurture Your Child's Developing Mind by Dr. Dan Siegel and Tina Payne Bryson, PhD

Positive Discipline books by Jane Nelsen, PhD, and her colleagues

Punished by Rewards: The Trouble with Gold Stars, Incentive Plans, A's, Praise, and Other Bribes by Alfie Kohn

Resilient: How to Grow an Unshakable Core of Calm, Strength, and Happiness by Rick Hanson, PhD, and Forrest Hanson

Self-Reg: How to Help Your Child (and You) Break the Stress Cycle and Successfully Engage with Life by Dr. Stuart Shanker and Teresa H. Barker

The Strength Switch: How the New Science of Strength-Based Parenting Helps Your Child and Your Teen Flourish by Dr. Lea Waters

The Teenage Brain: A Neuroscientist's Survival Guide to Raising Adolescents and Young Adults by Frances E. Jensen and Amy Ellis Nutt

Websites

The Center for Nonviolent Communication: *cnvc.org*

Positive Discipline: *positivediscipline.com*

Raffi's site and course: *raffifoundation.org /take-the-course*

VIA Institute on Character: *viacharacter.org/character -strengths*

Songs and Videos

"Belly Breathe" by Common and Colbie Caillat: *youtube.com/watch?v= _mZbzDOpylA*

"Take a Breath" by Raffi: *raffifoundation.org/download /take-a-breath-song*

REFERENCES

Allen, Summer. "The Science of Gratitude." May 2018. ggsc.berkeley.edu/images/uploads/GGSC-JTF _White_Paper-Gratitude-FINAL.pdf?_ga=2.204011735 .657781653.1581998050-1881279285.1578778213.

American Academy of Child and Adolescent Psychiatry. "Teen Brain: Behavior, Problem Solving, and Decision Making." February, 2020. aacap.org/AACAP/Families _and_Youth/Facts_for_Families/FFF-Guide/The-Teen -Brain-Behavior-Problem-Solving-and-Decision-Making -095.aspx.

Bath, Howard. "Calming Together: The Pathway to Self-Control." *Reclaiming Children and Youth: The Journal of Strength-Based Interventions* 16, no. 4 (2008): 44–46.

Baumrind, D. "The Influence of Parenting Style on Adolescent Competence and Substance Use." *The Journal of Early Adolescence* 11, no. 1 (1998): 56–95.

Benson, H., M. M. Greenwood, and H. Klemchuk. "The Relaxation Response: Psychophysiologic Aspects and Clinical Applications." *The International Journal of Psychiatry in Medicine* 6, no. 1 (1975): 87–98. doi.org /10.2190/376W-E4MT-QM6Q-H0UM.

Blakemore, Sarah-Jayne. *Inventing Ourselves: The Secret Life of the Teenage Brain.* New York: Public Affairs, 2018.

Burklund, L. J., J. D. Creswell, M. R. Irwin, and M. D. Lieberman. "The Common and Distinct Neural Bases of Affect Labeling and Reappraisal in Healthy Adults." *Frontiers in Psychology* 5 (2014): 221. doi.org/10.3389/fpsyg.2014.00221.

Carskadon, Mary A., Cecilia Vieira, and Christine Acebo. "Association between Puberty and Delayed Phase Preference." *Sleep* 16, no. 3 (1993): 258–262.

Cozolino, Louis. *The Neuroscience of Human Relationships: Attachment and the Developing Brain.* New York: W. W. Norton, 2002.

Devore, E. R., and K. R. Ginsburg. "The Protective Effects of Good Parenting on Adolescents." *Current Opinion in Pediatrics* 17, no. 4 (2005): 460–465.

Doskoch, Peter, and Angela Pirisi. "Why Tots Can't Play By the Rules." *Psychology Today.* Last reviewed June 9, 2016. psychologytoday.com/ca/articles/199612/why-tots-cant-play-the-rules.

Durrant, Joan, E. "Positive Discipline in Everyday Parenting." Save The Children, Published 6/11/2013. resourcecentre.savethechildren.net/library/positive-discipline-everyday-parenting-pdep-fourth-edition.

Dweck, Carol. "Carol Dweck Revisits the 'Growth Mindset.'" *Education Week* 35, no. 05 (2015): 20, 24.

Dweck, Carol. "The Perils and Promises of Praise." *Educational Leadership* 65, no. 2 (2007): 34–39.

Dwyer, Carol, and Heather Carlson-Jaquez. "Using Praise to Enhance Student Resilience and Learning Outcomes." American Psychological Association. February, 2020. apa.org/education/k12/using-praise.

Emmons, R. A., and A. Mishra. "Why Gratitude Enhances Well-Being: What We Know, What We Need to Know." *In Designing Positive Psychology: Taking Stock and Moving Forward*, edited by Kennon M. Sheldon, Todd B. Kashdan, and Michael F. Steger, 248–262. Oxford University Press, 2011.

Farber, Adele, and Elaine Mazlish. *How to Talk So Kids Will Listen and Listen So Kids Will Talk* New York: Scribner, 2012.

Fowler, James H., and Nicholas A. Christakis. "Dynamic Spread of Happiness in a Large Social Network: Longitudinal Analysis Over 20 Years in the Framingham Heart Study." *British Medical Journal* 337 (2008): a2338.

Gerritsen, Roderik J. S., and Guido P. H. Band. "Breath of Life: The Respiratory Vagal Stimulation Model of Contemplative Activity." *Frontiers in Human Neuroscience* (October 9, 2018). doi.org/10.3389/fnhum.2018.00397.

Ginsburg, Kenneth R., and Martha M. Jablow. *Resilience in Children and Teens: Giving Kids Roots and Wings*. 3rd ed. Itasca, Illinois: American Academy of Pediatrics, 2014.

Goleman, Daniel. *Emotional Intelligence: Why It Can Matter More Than IQ*. New York: Bantam, 2006.

Gottman, John. *The Seven Principles for Making Marriage Work: A Practical Guide from the Country's Foremost Relationship Expert*. New York: Crown, 1999.

HealthLinkBC. "Growth and Development, Ages 6 to 10 Years." May 11, 2019. healthlinkbc.ca/health-topics/te6244.

Healy, J. M. *Your Child's Growing Mind: Brain Development and Learning from Birth to Adolescence*. New York: Harmony, 2004.

Jensen, Frances E., and Amy Ellis Nutt. *The Teenage Brain: A Neuroscientist's Survival Guide to Raising Adolescents and Young Adults*. New York: Harper, 2015.

Karson, Michael. "Punishment Doesn't Work." *Psychology Today*. January 14, 2014. psychologytoday.com/ca/blog/feeling-our-way/201401/punishment-doesnt-work.

Kohn, Alfie. *Punished by Rewards: The Trouble with Gold Stars, Incentive Plans, A's, Praise, and Other Bribes*. Boston: Mariner, 2018.

Lieberman, M.D. "Social Cognitive Neuroscience: A Review of Core Processes." *The Annual Review of Psychology* 58 (2007): 259–89.

Live Science Staff. "Why Teens Are Lousy at Chores." May 17, 2005. livescience.com/270-teens-lousy-chores.html.

Miller, Claire Cain. "The Relentlessness of Modern Parenting." *New York Times*. December 25, 2018. nytimes.com/2018/12/25/upshot/the-relentlessness-of-modern-parenting.html.

Mueller, Claudia M., and Carol S. Dweck. "Praise for Intelligence Can Undermine Children's Motivation and Performance." *Journal of Personality and Social Psychology* 75, no. 1 (1998): 33–52.

Neff, Kristin. "Definition of Self Compassion." Self-Compassion. self-compassion.org/the-three -elements-of-self-compassion-2.

Ontario Ministry of Children, Community, and Social Services. "On MY Way." Last modified December 18, 2017. children.gov.on.ca/htdocs/English/professionals /middleyears/onmyway/cognitive-development.aspx.

Pellissier, Hank. "Inside the Preschooler's Brain." Great Schools. September 18, 2019. greatschools.org/gk /articles/preschooler-brain-development.

Seligman, Martin. *Authentic Happiness: Using the New Positive Psychology to Realize Your Potential for Lasting Fulfillment*. New York: Free Press, 2002.

Seligman, M. E. P., and M. Csikszentmihalyi. "Positive Psychology: An Introduction." *American Psychologist* 55, no. 1 (2000): 7.

Shanker, Stuart, and Teresa H. Barker. *Self-Reg: How to Help Your Child (and You) Break the Stress Cycle and Success-fully Engage with Life*. New York: Penguin, 2016.

Siegel, Dan, and Tina Payne Bryson. *No-Drama Discipline: The Whole-Brain Way to Calm the Chaos and Nurture Your Child's Developing Mind*. New York: Bantam, 2014.

Seigel, Dan and Tina Payne Bryson, *The Whole Brain Child: 12 Revolutionary Strategies to Nurture Your Child's Developing Mind*. New York: Bantam, 2016.

Stanford Children's Health. "Understanding the Teen Brain." February, 2020. stanfordchildrens.org/en/topic/default?id =understanding-the-teen-brain-1-3051.

University of California, Los Angeles. "Putting Feelings into Words Produces Therapeutic Effects in the Brain." *ScienceDaily*. June 22, 2007. sciencedaily.com/releases /2007/06/070622090727.htm.

Waters, Lea. *The Strength Switch: How the New Science of Strength-Based Parenting Helps Your Child and Your Teen Flourish*. New York: Avery, 2017.

INDEX

REFLECTIONS

REFLECTIONS

_____

_____

_____

_____

_____

_____

_____

_____

_____

_____

_____

_____

_____

_____

_____

_____

_____

_____

_____

ACKNOWLEDGMENTS

To Morgan: I am so grateful to you for trusting me with this project and letting me share my voice in such a meaningful way. Thank you for giving me a chance to be of service to others.

To Rachel: Thank you for your ongoing support, love, and excitement about every new project and idea I tell you about. I love sharing our lives with each other, even if it has to be from a distance.

To Alan: For the white-tailed deer and sideways moments specifically and all the support more generally. Thank you for being a friend.

To Cam: My love, I am delighted to acknowledge you and how you support me always. I thank you for letting me work when I needed to work and rest when I needed to rest (even though we both know I ended up working most of the time I said I would rest). I love you for always.

And to Aria, my lovey and sweet pea: Thank you for letting me write about us and share some of our stories and explorations. I feel like it's worth it, if only so I could mention our love of *Harry Potter* and the fact that you're part vampire and part cheetah just a few more times. You've taught me more about positive parenting than any book ever could. I love you more than the number of planets that can fit in the sun, times a billion. And then some more. And then a zillion heaps on top of that.

ABOUT THE AUTHOR

Dr. Nicole Libin is a certified mindfulness educator, adjunct professor, and author of *Sticky Brains* (a mindfulness and neuroplasticity storybook for kids), *Mindful Parenting in a Chaotic World*, and *5-Minute Mindfulness Meditations for Teens*. She has led mindfulness workshops, classes, and retreats for adults, adolescents, and children, and anyone else who will let her stop and take a breath with them. Nicole has taught and designed mindfulness curricula and other courses for Mindful Schools, Mount Royal University, and private organizations. She seeks to help others remember that it's okay not to be okay and works to offer specific, doable tools to cultivate compassion, focus, peace, and well-being . . . one breath at a time.

Nicole lives in Calgary with her husband, Cam, and her daughter, Aria, both of whom love salted caramel ice cream, *Harry Potter*, impromptu dance parties, and unicorns.

CPSIA information can be obtained
at www.ICGtesting.com
Printed in the USA
JSHW051007290820
7535JS00003BA/7